Knowledge

KEYWORDS IN TEACHER EDUCATION

SERIES EDITOR: VIV ELLIS

Taking cultural theorist Raymond Williams's concept as an organizing device, the Keywords in Teacher Education series offers short, accessibly written books on the most pressing and challenging ideas in the field.

Teacher education has a high profile in public policy and professional debates given the enduring associations between how teachers are prepared and how well their students do in school. At the same time, research perspectives on the important topics in the field are increasingly polarized with important consequences for the kind of teacher and the qualities of teaching that are most valued. Written by internationally recognized experts, these titles offer analyses both of the historical emergence and the consequences of the different positions in these debates.

ALSO AVAILABLE IN THE SERIES:

Expertise, Jessica Gerrard and Jessica Holloway
Identity, Sarah Steadman
Quality, Clare Brooks
Communities, Kenneth M. Zeichner
Disadvantage, Jo Lampert, Mervi Kaukko, Jane Wilkinson and Rocío García-Carrión

Knowledge

STEVEN PUTTICK, VICTORIA ELLIOTT AND JENNI INGRAM

BLOOMSBURY ACADEMIC
LONDON • NEW YORK • OXFORD • NEW DELHI • SYDNEY

BLOOMSBURY ACADEMIC
Bloomsbury Publishing Plc
50 Bedford Square, London, WC1B 3DP, UK
1385 Broadway, New York, NY 10018, USA
29 Earlsfort Terrace, Dublin 2, Ireland

BLOOMSBURY, BLOOMSBURY ACADEMIC and the Diana logo are
trademarks of Bloomsbury Publishing Plc

First published in Great Britain 2024

Cover design by Charlotte James
Cover image © Zoonar GmbH / Alamy Stock Photo

A catalogue record for this book is available from the British Library.

Library of Congress Control Number: 2024933918

ISBN: HB: 978-1-3503-3654-4
PB: 978-1-3503-3653-7
ePDF: 978-1-3503-3655-1
eBook: 978-1-3503-3656-8

Series: Keywords in Teacher Education

Typeset by Deanta Global Publishing Services, Chennai, India
Printed and bound in Great Britain

To find out more about our authors and books visit www.bloomsbury.com
and sign up for our newsletters.

CONTENTS

FIGURE

SERIES EDITOR'S FOREWORD

This series is organized by the concept of 'keywords', first elaborated by Welsh cultural theorist Raymond Williams (1976), and books in the series will seek to problematize and unsettle the ostensibly unproblematic and settled vocabulary of teacher education. From Williams' perspective, keywords are words and phrases that occur frequently in speech and writing, allowing conversation to ensue, but that nonetheless reveal profound differences in meaning within and across cultures, politics and histories. In teacher education, such keywords include practice, knowledge, quality and expertise. The analysis of such keywords allows us to trace the evolution of the emergent – and the maintenance of residual – meanings in teacher education discourses and practices. By analysing keywords, therefore, it is possible to elucidate the range of meanings of what Gallie (1955) referred to as 'essentially contested concepts' but in ways that promote a critical, historical understanding of changes in the fields in which they occur.

In the first edition of *Keywords*, Williams included entries on 108 units, ranging from 'Aesthetic' to 'Work'. A second edition followed in 1983 and other writers have subsequently used the concept to expand on Williams' original collection (e.g. Bennett et al., 2005; MacCabe & Yanacek, 2018) or to apply the concept to specific domains (e.g. A Community of Inquiry, 2018). This series applies it to teacher education. The purpose of the series mirrors that of Williams' original project: to trace ideological differences and social conflicts over time as they relate to the discourses and practices of a field (here, teacher education) by focusing on a selection of the field's high frequency words. So Keywords in Teacher Education is not a multi-volume dictionary.

The kind of analysis required by a focus on keywords goes beyond etymology or historical semantics. By selecting and analysing keywords, Williams argued:

> we find a history and complexity of meanings; conscious changes, or consciously different uses; innovation, obsolescence, specialization, extension, overlap, transfer; or changes which are masked by a nominal continuity so that words which seem to have been there for centuries, with continuous general meanings, have come in fact to express radically different or radically variable, yet sometimes hardly noticed, meanings and implications of meaning. (Williams, 1976, p. 17)

Given the increasingly strong attention paid to teacher education in education policy and in public debates about education more generally, focusing on keywords in this field is both timely and necessary. Uncovering and unsettling differences and conflicts in the vocabulary of preparing teachers renders the political and social bases underlying policy formation and public discourse more visible and therefore more capable of being acted upon.

Through this organizing device, the Keywords in Teacher Education series addresses the most important topics and questions in teacher education currently. It is a series of short books written in a direct and accessible style, each book taking one keyword as its point of departure and closely examining its cultural meanings historically while, crucially, identifying the social forces and material consequences of the differences and conflicts in meaning. Written by internationally recognized researchers, each peer-reviewed book offers cutting-edge analysis of the keyword underpinned by a deep knowledge of the available research within the field – and beyond it. One of the aims of the series is to broaden the gaze of teacher education research by engaging more systematically with the relevant humanities and social science literature – to acknowledge, as Williams did, that our understanding is deepened and has the potential for action strengthened by seeking to understand the social relations between words, texts and the multiple contexts in which their meanings are produced.

Knowledge is perhaps one of the pre-eminent keywords in contemporary discourses of teacher education. The phrase 'knowledge-rich' has become a slogan and a rallying-cry as well as an argument. Knowledge is positioned in distinction to skills as well as information in contemporary educational debates as well as more fundamental questions of what is knowledge/not-knowledge. Puttick, Elliott and Ingram delve into these debates in their contribution to the series by addressing two main dimensions of the consequential impact of knowledge as a keyword in teacher education: first, what knowledge means and how teachers are prepared to teach children knowledge derived from subject disciplines; second, what knowledge do teachers need to know in order to teach effectively and that therefore needs to be included as 'content' in their initial teacher education programs. Along the way, how knowledge is described and explained becomes consequential – whether it has volume and a material presence (building up knowledge 'brick by brick') or whether it exists in a set of discipline-based social relations (Ellis, 2006).

Drawing on a range of educational research from the 1970s to the present day, the authors provide an overview of the contested terrain of knowledge in teacher education. They consider key epistemological questions as well as those of education policy – and why knowledge has become such a powerful keyword in teacher education today. Knowledge is also considered in relation to decolonization, at the same time as concepts such as 'core knowledge' and (mono-) 'cultural literacy' have come to be so influential in English education policy, particularly. The role of knowledge in initial teacher education programs is also considered – and how teachers might become part of discipline-based communities of practice with deep 'subject knowledge' rather than simply a 'professional knowledge recipe' (Ellis, 2007). At a time when teachers, teacher educators and parents/carers are urged to 'bring knowledge back in', this latest contribution to the series questions what exactly that means.

Viv Ellis

Melbourne, 2023

References

A Community of Inquiry (2018). *Keywords; for further consideration and particularly relevant to academic life, especially as it concerns disciplines, inter-disciplinary endeavor and modes of resistance to the same.* Princeton, NJ: Princeton University Press.

Bennett, T., Grossberg, L., & Morris, M. (2005). *New keywords. A revised vocabulary of culture and society.* Oxford: Blackwell Publishing.

Ellis, V. (2006). *Subject knowledge and teacher education: The development of beginning teachers' thinking.* London and New York: Continuum.

Ellis, V. (2007). Taking subject knowledge seriously: From professional knowledge recipes to complex conceptualisations of teacher development. *The Curriculum Journal, 18*(3), 447–62.

Gallie, W. B. (1955). Essentially contested concepts. *Proceedings of the Aristotelian Society, 56,* 167–98.

McCabe, C., Yanacek, H., & the Keywords Project. (2018). *Keywords for today. A 21st century vocabulary.* Oxford: Oxford University Press.

Williams, R. (1976). *Keywords: A vocabulary of culture and society.* London: Fontana.

CHAPTER 1

Introduction

Raymond Williams' (1985) analysis of 'keywords' that inspires this series creates space to critically examine how we speak, write, research, practice and debate the endlessly fascinating area of teacher education. In this contribution we examine the keyword 'knowledge'. Part of Williams' (1985) aim was to open some of the variations and tensions that exist between the ways in which we use these keywords. This opening up makes us more aware of the 'different immediate values or different kinds of valuation' we associate with the word, and of the 'different formations and distributions of energy and interest' (Williams, 1985, p. 12). His own analysis of the multiple, contested and shifting constellations of meanings associated with various keywords reveals significant differences, 'especially when strong feelings or important ideas are in question' (p.12). While 'knowledge' was not given a separate entry in Williams' own *Keywords*, it features heavily in his discussion of philosophy, experience, positivism and nature, often framed as something produced through scientific experiments and observation, or by reasoning through principles and ideas. He also notes that the earliest uses of the term 'science' was 'a term for knowledge as such' (p.196) that was used in ways that distinguish between theoretical and practical knowledges. These distinctions find their own articulations – some novel, others strongly echoing older debates – in teacher education today as different formations and distributions of energy and interest shape what we mean by knowledge.

'Knowledge' is deeply embedded in discourse surrounding teacher education. Gerrard and Holloway's (2023) brilliant contribution to this series on Keywords in Teacher Education includes eighty references to knowledge, and the idea of knowledge has strong political dimensions bound up with fundamental questions about the aims of education. The substantial energies that have been devoted to debates about knowledge gesture to the shared belief in the importance of knowledge for teaching and teacher education. Questions about what knowledge should be taught – across schools and settings – and what knowledges teachers ought to be equipped with are all political and inherently contestable questions. There are a massive number of concepts, policies, procedures, techniques, principles and persons that teachers need to know. Most of these knowledges change over time and at different rates, which means that teachers' knowledge is not only massive but also dynamic. From policy changes to conceptual and substantive developments in subject disciplines, to the almost minute-by-minute shifts in their students' engagement, understanding and emotional states, the range of things that teachers are expected to know is staggering. These different knowledges are produced in very different ways, come from a wide range of sources and are known through multiple approaches. The examples of policies, subjects, pedagogies and persons relate to and feature procedural, affective, testimonial, explicit and implicit knowledges that teachers engage with by reading, listening, observing, feeling and more. One of our starting points in this book is that teachers' ability to manage these complex knowledges is amazing, and teacher education has an important and challenging role in supporting teachers to successfully navigate these knowledge environments.

Defining Knowledge

The challenges of defining knowledge can be illustrated by the ways in which different traditions have grappled with it. For example, in the sociology of education there are fascinating shifts revealed through Michael Young's attention to knowledge from the edited collection *Knowledge and Control* (1971) to, nearly forty years later, *Bringing Knowledge Back In* (2008). The later project is positioned as 'rescuing' (2000) knowledge from all kinds of 'bad' forces seeking to relativize or marginalize an educational focus on knowledge. Young's development of the concept 'powerful knowledge' has been a highly influential discourse in curriculum policy, theory and practice, and we return to this idea later in the book, particularly in Chapter 6. Young's definition of knowledge begins in negative terms: in his view it is *not* experience; nor is it opinions or common sense. Differentiation between types of knowledge is central to his account: 'in particular between the knowledge that pupils bring to school and the knowledge that the curriculum gives them access to. This view does not involve any esoteric distinctions, nor will it be wholly unfamiliar to readers of this book. Despite this it is all too often dismissed by educationalists' (Young et al., 2015, p. 14).

Polemical rhetoric reducing complex issues to simplistic positions cuts across multiple interventions surrounding the place of knowledge in education, simplistic dichotomies between knowledge and experience, and dividing people into homogenous groups. For example, between 'progressive' and 'traditional', or here between 'educationalists' and others. Their negative qualification ('does not involve any esoteric distinctions') is an interesting way of sidestepping problematic questions around how we might define knowledge. Does 'esoteric' here mean that we are free to ignore philosophical discussion of knowledge? There is also an intriguing paradox between the way their account holds up 'powerful' disciplinary knowledge as the gold standard to which schools ought to give students access, and the way in which their central concept is defined through appeals to common sense and in opposition to disciplinary (philosophical) insights into knowledge. This brief example illustrates the inherently contestable nature of discussions about knowledge, and the ways in which the conceptual complexity has been addressed and popularized. It also hints at the fraught relationship between policymakers, practitioners, curriculum and disciplinary knowledges. On the one hand, knowledge produced in disciplines is seen as the highest form of knowledge, yet its power is problematic: those with power may not want certain truths being spoken to them, while those popularizing simplistic categories may also not want them to be troubled (hence, the dismissal of philosophical analytic rigour as 'esoteric').

Before we go any further, we will offer a definition of *knowledge* which, drawing from a philosophical perspective (and 'virtue epistemology' in particular), defines knowledge as: 'belief arising out of acts of intellectual virtue' (Zagzebski, 1999, p. 109), and this definition is extended to include both propositional knowledge and knowledge gained through experience or 'acquaintance': knowledge is 'cognitive contact with reality arising out of acts of intellectual virtue' (p.109).

This definition stands in stark opposition to, for example, an economic rationale – explored further later – in which knowledge is seen as a commodity that can be parcelled up and sold. Knowledge as 'cognitive contact with reality arising out of acts of intellectual virtue' raises many fascinating questions for teacher education and curricula: What 'kinds of reality'? Whose reality? In what ways might the curriculum best represent and give access to 'reality'? Assumptions about knowledge as something that can be commodified and primarily held within people contrasts with the ways in which many researchers understand knowledge as something developing and achieving value among or between people (Ellis, 2007; Ingram, 2018). Zagzebski's (1999) definition also highlights differences between assumptions about knowledge as mainly a technical, mechanical thing and process, against something with which persons relate to, engage with and are responsible for, and so this understanding of knowledge is also social:

> We tend to think of knowledge as our own accomplishment, but this is rarely the case. The fact that our knowledge depends upon the knowledge and intellectual virtue of a host of other persons in our intellectual community, as well as a cooperating universe, makes it clear that we cannot expect to isolate the conditions for knowledge in some set of independent properties of the knower, much less a set of properties over which the knower has control. (p.109)

What are the 'particular circumstances' of teaching and of teacher education? How do they change across time and space, and how might teacher educators best prepare teachers to engage with these dynamic knowledges? Who is a part of these intellectual communities? Who has what power, and who is excluded? An important tradition of work, often referred to as 'decolonial', has asked critical questions about the dominance of Anglo-American knowledge production. It speaks back to the assumption mentioned earlier that knowledge is a 'great good' by arguing for both its 'shine' and its 'shadow'. We draw on this tradition to raise a series of interconnected questions about representation, knowledge production and the construction of canons and curricula (Elliott, 2020); questions that foreground the relationships between knowledge and power.

What has often been referred to as the 'social construction of knowledge' draws our attention to knowledge as a concept and to the ways in which this concept is produced: what the idea of knowledge is considered to be, how the term is used and what the effects of these different constructions and uses are. The term 'knowledge' has played an important role in the ways that education has been imagined and debated. But what is knowledge? Who gets to define it? Who decides what counts as knowledge? How we understand and use the concept is contested and inherently political: there is no neutral knowledge, and neither is the concept itself neutral. Part of our hope in this book is to examine how the idea of knowledge functions discursively across a range of teacher education contexts. Across policy discourses, curriculum studies and teacher education praxis, knowledge has been used in different ways to serve very different ends, foregrounding questions about the nature and value of knowledge.

Knowledge and Money

What kind of a thing is knowledge? Whatever else it may be, knowledge is widely seen to be good – and more than that, it is seen to be a 'great good' (Zagzebski, 1999, p. 100). But what counts as 'good'? Is knowledge a natural, single kind of thing, for example, like gold? Or is it multiple and constructed? Asking about an equivalence with gold draws our attention to the commercialization and reduction of knowledge to a commodity that can be owned and sold. One powerful narrative about knowledge has tied it directly to money, and the OECD's (Organisation for Economic Co-operation and Development) report *The Knowledge-Based Economy* (OECD, 1996) offers an influential statement of an economic perspective on knowledge. They construct an idea of knowledge as a commodity that can be measured and tracked through inputs, flows and outputs. Such an understanding positions education at the 'centre of the knowledge-based economy, and learning the tool of individual and organisational advancement' (p.14). These economies are 'directly based on the production, distribution and use of knowledge and information' (p.14), and, driven by these assumptions, schools take on particular functions in service of the economy, tying students' education to the amount of knowledge they can retain and contribute to the economy. These ideas about knowledge and education are made particularly obvious in discussions about how much different degrees are 'worth', with the value of their worth being calculated using students' future earnings and contribution to the economy. For example, in an English context, the Office for Students describes its aim as ensuring that universities and colleges are 'offering real value for money and giving graduates the best chance of fulfilling careers that contribute to our shared prosperity' (OFS, 2022). The easy proxy of future earnings has been used to categorize subjects as 'high' and 'low' value, with the 'lower value' courses being mockingly referred to in the press as 'Mickey Mouse' degrees (Evening Standard, 2022). Gaining a 'decent job' on graduation means earning above a certain amount. Among other things, the exchange value of the subject knowledge is determined by how much money someone with that degree is paid. These economic ideas about knowledge create a powerful and influential narrative, and the assumptions that come bundled with it of knowledge as a thing and as a commodity, are returned to throughout our discussion of knowledge in teacher education. But how might we define *knowledge*?

Knowledge and Power

How knowledge might be *used* in teacher education raises philosophical and practical questions about the nature of teaching and the relationships between school subjects and academic disciplines. Introducing beginning teachers to the complex and contested knowledges they must engage with is an exciting, challenging and unavoidably political task: among other things, it is about power over knowledge production and circulation. The breadth of interdisciplinary knowledges that teacher educators draw on places them in a position of 'epistemic dependence' (Castree, 2014): we are often reliant on the ideas, claims and knowledges of others. Similarly, school students are reliant on the knowledge of their teachers. The circulation, development and refinement of knowledge is inherently social and is shot through with asymmetrical power relations. Drawing on decolonial critiques of the 'shadow and shine' of knowledge (Rudolph et al., 2018), and asking 'what kind of knowledge, by whom, what for' (Mignolo, 2011, p. xvi), we develop a notion of *knowledge for all*. Mignolo's (2011) central aim in *The Darker Side of Western Modernity: Global Futures, Decolonial Options* is:

> To dispel the myth that there are global needs but only one (diverse) center where knowledge is produced to solve the problem of every body, and to contribute to breaking the Western code, [Mignolo argues] that the anchor of decolonial epistemologies shall be 'I am where I think' and better yet 'I am where I do and think' . . . [which means that] you constitute yourself ('I am') in the place you think. And that place is not, in my argument, a room or office at the library, but the 'place' that has been configured by the colonial matrix of power. (p. xvi)

By drawing attention to where knowledge is produced, by whom and for what purposes, Mignolo reveals the historic inequalities of power and knowledge; uncovering the presumptions of knowledge produced some-where that portrayed itself to the world as a view from no-where or every-where. In doing this work of revealing and uncovering, Mignolo's argument also functions to open up horizons, expanding whose knowledge gets to contribute to these global discourses. Teacher education suffers from the same Anglo-American dominance, and the teaching profession suffers from classed, racialized and gendered issues (Bhopal & Rhamie, 2014; Lander, 2011) that make questions about the kinds of knowledges that are included (and excluded) urgent. We return to these questions from multiple perspectives across the book, critically exploring ongoing conversations in different subject traditions across multiple international contexts.

Structure of the Book

Chapter 2 situates the discussions firmly within the context of young people in schools and the kinds of knowledge they might be given access to. It opens debates about the nature of knowledge, particularly disciplinary knowledge. The relationships between subjects and between subjects and academic disciplines are examined through the cases of English, science, mathematics and geography (Puttick, 2015; Elliott, 2020). We use the differing epistemologies of the three authors to explore questions such as: What is the nature of knowledge in different school subjects? How does the nature of knowledge in school differ from the nature of knowledge studied and researched in universities? What is the role of teacher educators and teacher education in managing the interface between subjects and disciplines? Disciplinary knowledge is often contested and uncertain, yet it is often treated as uncontested and certain when taught in the classroom. Disciplinary knowledge develops over time through challenge and debate and needs to re-contextualized from academic to school settings. These processes of transformation raise challenging issues around the extent to which subject studies in schools should or could reflect the disciplinary approaches to these subjects beyond school. Finally, this chapter considers the relationships between knowledge in school and knowledge in pupils' everyday lives. To what extent does the knowledge pupils need for their examinations prepare them for the knowledge they will need in their everyday lives, both now and in the future?

Chapter 3 then explores the terminology of knowledge, information, skills and understanding, and the debates about their relative priority in education. We consider the ways in which knowledge functions discursively in these debates, and in particular the constructed dichotomy between knowledge and skills, and how that relates to beliefs about the purpose of education, such as rhetorical links to social mobility via a certain conception of cultural capital, or a focus on the preparation of students for future employment. Challenges to the importance of knowledge come from the ubiquity of technology. Using this context we explore the difference between knowledge and information, and the skills required to interpret what is discovered via Google. The function of algorithms in search engines drives the visibility (or non-visibility) of some information and knowledge in searches, reproducing and reinforcing real-world biases (Noble, 2018; Amoore, 2020). We discuss how this affects teachers' searches for knowledge via the internet, and how various disciplines can and have challenged the substitution of the internet for real engagement with knowledge (Wineburg, 2018). The difference between knowledge and information is then used to consider the influence of cognitive psychology on teaching today, and to explore the impact that the use of 'knowledge organizers' and retrieval practice can have on the ways in which knowledge is framed in the classroom. The kinds of information which are easily utilized in these popular approaches creates a bias towards low-level factual knowledge rather than deep engagement with disciplinary understanding and knowledge (Elliott, 2020).

Chapter 4 then moves to ask: What types of knowledge are most important for teaching? What does it mean for teachers to know-that, know-how, know-why and know-to? The different conceptions of teacher knowledge or knowing, drawing from a range of theoretical perspectives introduced in Chapter 2, reveal the complexity of finding an answer to these questions. This complexity is compounded by similarities and differences between discipline-specific conceptions, and the relationship between theory and practice. Beginning with Winch, Oancea and Orchards' (2015) interconnected and complementary aspects of teachers' professional knowledge, this chapter considers how teachers develop the knowledge(s) they need. Examining a range of models and theories of teacher learning and growth, both during initial teacher education and extending beyond, we analyse a range of arguments around the roles of and relationships between theory, practice and contexts. In particular, we discuss the roles of critical reflection, practical theorizing (McIntyre, 1995) and teacher noticing (Schack et al., 2017) in the development of teacher knowledge.

The relations between power and knowledge – particularly as developed in the discourse surrounding *powerful knowledge* (Young et al., 2014) – are the focus of Chapter 5. Internationally, powerful knowledge has gained substantial traction, often in combination with notions of cultural capital and cultural literacy, to address the question: What knowledge is most worth teaching? Based on distinctions between different types of knowledge, including *everyday/disciplinary* and *knowledge of the powerful/powerful knowledge*, powerful knowledge sets out to establish what knowledge is most valuable for students to learn, often in relation to claims about social justice. This chapter analyses the functions of powerful knowledge in policy discourses across a range of international cases, and it then moves to examine critiques of powerful knowledge, including conceptual and definitional issues (White, 2019) – particularly the nature of powerful knowledge as a 'cluster concept'; the 'shadow and shine' of knowledge (Rudolph et al., 2018); and through subject-specific critiques of the foundational dichotomies on which powerful knowledge is made, particularly in distinguishing between everyday and powerful knowledges. Drawing on Rudolph et al.'s (2018) use of the 'shadow and shine' of knowledge to critically examine the relations between power and knowledge, and the problematic features of powerful knowledge policy discourses identified through this chapter, it expands on the discussion about subjects and disciplines in Chapter 2 to pose the question: Should we be talking about *disciplinary literacy* instead? The chapter concludes by exploring the potential of disciplinary literacy to expand discourse, policy and practice in ways that may currently be restricted by ideas about powerful knowledge.

Attention to the 'shadow and shine' of knowledge in Chapter 5 argues that the inherently social nature of knowledge production foregrounds questions around who defines what knowledge is valuable. Recent developments have expanded who might be included within the curriculum, and in Chapter 6 we utilize the case of women authors as part of the English canon as a way to examine shifts in accepted curricular knowledge. What might we learn from these shifts for research and practice in teacher education? In what ways might these past curricular shifts illuminate contemporary opportunities and challenges for constructing curriculum that are diverse, inclusive and accessible for all? In the context of teacher education (Bhopal & Rhamie, 2014), and higher education more broadly (Roth & Ritter, 2021), structural inequalities are deeply embedded in the production of white and settler colonial discourses (McKittrick, 2021; Patel, 2016). Internationally, and across many subjects, attention has more recently been given to asking: Why is my curriculum so white (Esson, 2020)? Distinctions between *what* and *whose* knowledge are complicated by the powerful ways in which Black and Indigenous scholars of colour continue to be under-represented and under-cited in relation to their white colleagues. In this chapter we review a range of recent interventions seeking to expand the kinds of knowledges produced through and worked with in teacher education. Thinking across a range of subjects and different settings of practice, this chapter sets an ambitious vision of knowledge for all.

The final chapter (7) locates the discussion from the rest of the book firmly in the realm of teacher education practice. We begin by arguing for an expansion of the knowledges which are given attention in teacher education, and grounding that attention throughout the initial teacher education curriculum. The practice of teacher educators could and should be adapted in order to enable teachers to critically engage with debates on knowledge and skills, and rhetoric around both, throughout their careers. As a result, this chapter also encourages readers – and all teachers – to reflect critically on the kinds of knowledge we value. Another consequence of the more expansive conception of knowledge that we have argued for is a need to embrace a greater level of complexity about knowledge. We also consider the potential of teacher education and teachers' ongoing engagement with their own education for the creation of new knowledges (knowledge for teaching, knowledge in action, etc.) in each moment in the classroom, and more broadly within the discipline. We end by reflecting on implications of disciplinary knowledge epistemologies for the development of educational/social scientific epistemologies and the potential consequences for teachers and teacher educators.

CHAPTER 2

Subjects, Disciplines and Knowledge

As we start this chapter, we invite you to imagine a student – Kai – who has just started secondary school. After spending twenty minutes with their form group, Kai moves quickly to a mathematics lesson. Algebra today. After an hour of mathematics, they walk across the school to the languages department where they are greeted with a colourful display 'Hola! Bonjour! Hallo!' and then go into their Mandarin lesson, focusing on greetings. After an hour of Mandarin they have twenty minutes outside for breaktime. Time for a snack and to catch up with friends. Then past the world map and photographs from last year's fieldwork visits and Kai has geography where they are learning about glaciation. Next they have English, where they are studying Macbeth. Then lunchtime, and today Kai has hockey practice which means a quick sandwich on the way, change into kit and then training for the rest of the hour. After the warm up they do passing drills for twenty minutes and then play a game. After a quick shower and change Kai goes to the final lesson of the day: chemistry, where they are learning about the structure of atoms. Across this day there are at least four different rapid switches between subjects and the associated approaches for thinking about what it means to 'know', between understandings of what words like 'explanation' mean when different teachers ask for them, and between ideas of what 'a right answer' could look like, all within a single short day.

The majority of secondary teachers have a particular specialism in one subject discipline, on the basis of a single epistemological understanding of what knowledge is. In secondary, middle or high schools, it is all too easy to forget that students in school switch rapidly between subjects, having to fundamentally shift their mental conceptions of what knowledge is and on what basis it can be justified. In primary schools, teachers often have to make these shifts too. They may have studied a range of subjects if they entered the profession via an undergraduate degree leading to a primary teaching qualification. They may have studied one of the subject disciplines taught in schools followed by a postgraduate teaching qualification, or they may have studied education as a social science before studying for a teaching qualification (or any number of other combinations). This is where epistemology – the area of philosophy concerned with the nature and justification of knowledge – becomes particularly relevant to teacher education. Epistemological inquiry is guided by three broad questions: What are the limits of human knowledge? What are the sources of human knowledge? And, what is the nature of human knowledge? (Arner, 1972). Hofer and Pintrich frame personal epistemologies as being 'how individuals come to know, the theories and beliefs they hold about knowing, and the manner in which such epistemological premises are a part of and an influence on the cognitive processes of thinking and reasoning' (1997, p. 8). The personal epistemologies of teachers can be very influential on the ways in which knowledge is framed in lessons for students. In English, the characteristic pedagogies of communal reading of a text and then discussion of that text tell us about how we construct knowledge (i.e. the epistemological basis of the subject) (Elliott, 2020) – we base it on textual detail, and we construct knowledge in interaction with others, whether that is other people in the classroom, the text itself, writers about the text, teachers outside the classroom and so on. In a mathematics lesson, meanwhile, Kai's experience might depend on the particular epistemological position of their teacher. The kinds of instruction in which students are immersed 'parallel' the epistemological beliefs they develop. Epistemology within mathematics is more contested: Is knowledge absolute, unified and fixed, existing independently of people, or is it socially constructed and something that you do? Is school maths about the development of logical thinking, abstraction and rigor? A toolbox that students can use (both in other subject areas and in life)? Is it problem solving? (Watson, 2008). These questions seem to apply equally across phases of education, and there is an extensive body of research on how the epistemological beliefs of primary teachers affects their students' learning of mathematics (e.g. Newton & Newton, 2008; Felbrich et al., 2014). Moving to a geography lesson, Kai might be taken out of the classroom so they can 'actually see' the world: an epistemology that is based on empirical, experiential knowledge that is best experienced first-hand. In the geography classroom, geographical enquiry (Roberts, 2013) plays an important role in the construction of knowledge and of our ideas about how we come to know in geography. In geographical enquiry, we base knowledge on a wide range of evidence that prioritizes data from the 'real world' that are illuminated through geographical concepts. Again, the epistemological challenges associated with the kinds of knowledge being learnt across phases of education are very similar – in this example, thinking about geographical enquiry in very similar ways across primary and secondary education. This kind of enquiry is intentionally open-ended. It will conclude with answers to the questions driving it, but it also looks forward by stimulating more questions: knowledge here is seen as dynamic, generative and creative, and also open to revision.

This chapter opens and situates debates about the nature of knowledge, specifically disciplinary knowledge. The relationships between subjects, and between subjects and the academic disciplines are examined through the cases of

English, mathematics and geography (Elliott, 2020; Ingram & Andrews, 2019; Puttick, 2015). In some ways, this chapter introduces content knowledge aspects of teacher knowledge, and extends this to consider the disciplinary knowledge or ways of knowing and being. In many subjects, disciplinary knowledge is contested and uncertain yet it is often treated as uncontested and certain when taught in the classroom. In these subjects, disciplinary knowledge develops over time through challenge and debate and needs to be re-contextualized (Bernstein, 1999) from an academic setting to a school one. In other subjects such as mathematics (Ernest, 1989), there is little uncertainty around the facts and content of the curriculum, but what it means to do mathematics is heavily contested and it is this aspect that needs recontextualizing. These complex questions about recontextualization between subjects and disciplines raise some challenging issues around the extent to which subject studies in schools should or could reflect the disciplinary approaches to these subjects beyond school. The disciplinary boundaries may be less obvious in a primary classroom, particularly in the earlier years, where project-based learning may develop knowledge in multiple areas, growing geographical knowledge, scientific knowledge and literacy through a weather topic, for example.

Epistemology – What Is It?

Epistemology asks the question: How can we know something? It moves from ontological questions of 'what is there to be known' to more pragmatic ones – how can we measure something, how can we describe it, what counts as evidence for it? Within the field of educational research, there are a huge number of disciplines represented – sociology, psychology, anthropology, history, economics and others (Furlong, 2013). This variety of disciplines means that different educational knowledge comes from different epistemological backgrounds. Among practitioners, teachers of different subjects may be drawn to different types of educational research (the anthropological, the phenomenological, the statistical evidence of the Randomised Controlled Trial) because of their own personal epistemological backgrounds. Among the authors of this book we have very different disciplinary backgrounds represented; geography, literature and mathematics. Victoria, a former English teacher, understands knowledge in literature as being constructed in dialogue with texts and others, 'produced through argument with others whether real or imagined, as we work through possible interpretations' (Elliott, 2020, p. 13). Knowledge in literature also draws on some 'real' things: 'dates, information about authors, real geographical locations, truly identifiable literary techniques and so on' (Elliott, 2022, p. 17). This background shapes her epistemological position in educational knowledge, which relies on the construction of argument with detailed reference to data, where individual people's perceptions of their reality are important, but there are some underlying non-relative facts. (This largely aligns with a critical realist epistemology.) This can be characterized as Victoria's 'epistemological world view'.

Jenni, a former mathematics teacher, sees mathematics as a collection of theorems, definitions and proofs. This knowledge has been firmly established many years ago and rarely changes. Occasionally theorems and definitions evolve to include or omit new cases, but innovation and development in mathematical research very rarely affects the mathematical content taught in schools (or often universities). Mathematical concepts, structures and relationships are mostly abstract, with real-world approximations serving mainly as an incomplete representation. While mathematical modelling is an essential tool in many other subjects, the beauty is in the abstraction, not the application. Some of these features carry through into Jenni's educational research, such as the fascination in the unobservable and the awareness of the role and limitations of mathematical or statistical models.

Steve, a former geography teacher, understands knowledge in geography through a similar (to Victoria) 'critical realist' epistemology which is expansive and draws widely across physical and human geographies. Geographical knowledge is both constructed socially and is also about things (whether material, non-material and so on) that exist external to those people and their perceptions and grasp of them. This position might be illustrated through Jazeel's (2021) discussion in *The 'City' as Text*. The quote marks around 'City' hint at his provocation, and he argues that spatial concepts – of which 'City' is an example – are 'as epistemological as they are material and real' (p. 660). Research on climate change education offers an example of this approach towards knowledge (Puttick et al., 2022): climate change is seen as being 'as epistemological' as it is material and real, which means that how the idea of climate change is understood – what meanings it takes on, what discourses it produces, what imaginaries it makes possible and what options it shuts down – is vital for research to explore (and this would equally apply to related concepts such as Anthropocene and climate crisis). But climate change is also more than these knowledges *about* it.

Beyond the general world view, people also hold differing epistemological beliefs about different dimensions of knowledge, such as simplicity, certainty, justification and inception (Schraw et al., 2012). Certainty of knowledge refers to 'the extent to which knowledge is viewed as fixed or fluid. An individual may consider knowledge to be existing with certainty. In such cases, knowledge cannot be doubted, all experts would come up with the same answer to a question, and that answer would not change over time' (Guilfoyle et al., 2020, p. 3). We have already conceptualized much of teacher knowledge as dynamic, which lets you know where we stand on this dimension! We have also made our views on simplicity known, arguing that knowledge is complex. The origin of knowledge refers to the source – does it reside outside the learner, is it transmitted from authority and not permitted to be questioned, or is it constructed in interaction with others?

The following example from school geography illustrates one of the ways in which distinctive subject approaches to knowledge might be understood and described by teachers. This particular case also highlights the diversity of approaches that can be found within – as well as between – some subjects, an issue that is strongly felt in the distinctions between 'human' and 'physical' geography. At a disciplinary level these different sub-disciplines are associated with quite different research traditions, funding streams and assumptions about the nature of knowledge. Human geography is primarily associated with the social sciences, and physical geography with the natural sciences (although this simplification does hide some exciting work that is being done across – and to break down – these dichotomies, such as through *Critical Physical Geography*). There are distinctive journals (such as *Progress in Physical Geography* and *Progress in Human Geography*), and in some places separate departments and courses. Within the school subject, awarding bodies often present separate areas of physical and human geography within the examination specifications, and many secondary schools teach modules dedicated to fairly separate attention to physical and human geographies. The secondary school geography teacher in the example we now present was observed as part of a larger study on secondary school geography teachers' subject knowledge (Puttick, 2018). The teacher – Ruth – described herself as a physical geographer, and made strong claims for the primacy of physical geography over human geography, and also for geography over the subject of English literature. Geographical knowledge for Ruth is described later in terms of timeless archetypes combined with empirical verification. She described an English lesson in which she, as a sixth form student, was studying Keats' 'Ode to a Nightingale'. The aim of the lesson was to study the thought processes Keats had gone through in writing the poem.

> I'm thinking how do you know that? how d'you know he wasn't just . . . sat there thinking I need to knock out another poem [laughing] – what shall I write – oh, lets write about a nightingale! (Ruth, interview 1:22)

Keats calls a lady in his poem Ruth; the pseudonym this teacher went on to choose. Keats' Ruth has a sad heart which is passed through by the Nightingale's song as it flies

> Past the near meadows, over the still stream,
> Up the hill-side; and now 'tis buried deep
> In the next valley-glades:
> Was it a vision, or a waking dream?
> Fled is that music: – Do I wake or sleep?

(KEATS, 1977, p. 194)

For our Ruth, these questions are empirical, and obvious. She enthusiastically described the empirical, verifiable nature of geography in terms of physical proximity to the objects of study: being able to *actually see*. First-hand experience of physical features played a significant role in Ruth's decision to study geography at university, based around a 'strange pivotal moment' on a glaciated feature like a very small hill (called a Drumlin) in North Wales:

> I can remember the moment where the teacher actually said to us what's this? What's this feature we're on? . . . and then looking down and realising I was actually stood on a Drumlin, and going 'this is a Drumlin!' I'm in a glaciated valley – this is a Drumlin. This is just brilliant! I love this! (Puttick, 2015, pp. 130–1)

How you might explain these different things and concepts – drumlins, glaciation, poetry, meaning, affect – involves a wide range of contrasting approaches.

In mathematics, the differences between the kind of mathematics taught at university and the mathematics taught at school are well documented (Ernest, 1989; Watson, 2008), as are differences in the way that mathematics is taught (Ingram & Gorgen, 2020). At university, mathematics is often presented deductively, beginning with definitions and theorems which are then proved. At school, mathematics is often presented inductively, building on examples that are contextualized. There are similarities, yet there are also differences between the mathematics taught at university and the mathematics the researchers at the forefront of the field are doing (Burton, 2004). In English the distinctions between school and university are complex: English language (arts) becomes linguistics at university; literary study gains levels of complexity as students progress, in terms of increasing comfort with ambiguity, uncertainty and more complex theoretical understandings of texts. Snapper (2009) highlights that the expectations at university for greater independent ability to apply theoretical frameworks to texts, and indeed that students would encounter complex theoretical material and render it into a form they could use without support create major problems in the transition from school to university literary study. In geography, there are some notable differences in the substantive knowledge taught in school and at university, with feminist and decolonial perspectives being examples of areas receiving limited attention in school geography (Rose, 2020). There are also marked differences in the way that (un) certainty is dealt with: in school, geographical knowledge is often presented in highly certain terms, whereas in university the inherent uncertainty and situatedness of knowledge receives more attention. The ways in which certainty of subject knowledge is dealt with presents challenges for beginning teachers and the ways in which they navigate between being seen to have 'strong' subject knowledge while also acknowledging the tentativeness, limits and partiality of this same knowledge (Puttick, 2018).

Mathematics often deals with abstract ideas that are not necessarily connected to reality, such as numbers, variables and geometric relationships. We talk about the number 2 or a circle, but neither of these actually exist out there in reality. Some of these abstract ideas do not sit well with our everyday experiences. For example, there are the same number of whole numbers $(1, 2, 3, 4, \ldots)$ as there are even numbers $(2, 4, 6, 8, \ldots)$. Intuitively this does not match with our experiences, it seems 'obvious' that there will be twice as many whole numbers as even numbers since every even number can be made by doubling a whole number. However, mathematically we can pair each whole number with an even number through this doubling relationship, so 1 is paired with 2, 2 is paired with 4, 3 is paired with 6 and so on. This pairing continues for ever, and because every whole number can be paired with every even number so there are the same number of whole numbers as even numbers (what mathematicians call the same cardinality).

At school, students are likely to experience examples of these abstract ideas in contexts they can relate to, and students then need to navigate across these contexts. For example, a fraction can be seen as an object (the number one half, a point on a number line), it can also be seen as a process (half of a pizza), and the result of a calculation (1 divided by 2). It is often only at university level that this idea of fraction is defined in a way that is abstracted from each of these representations of a fraction.

It's also worth noting at this point that across the world there are tensions between Western epistemic beliefs – which tend to be promoted through formal schooling – and the epistemic world views of Indigenous peoples. The 'sustained effort to sever Indigenous peoples from traditional education and traditional knowledges' (via the promotion of Western-style educational norms) has been called 'epistemicide' (Wilson & Laing, 2018, p. 133). Indigenous, Aboriginal and Native epistemologies and ontologies are plural. There is no singular set of belief which is 'the Indigenous' viewpoint – but as we have been endeavouring to show, that is also true of Western epistemologies. We pick up on Indigenous knowledge in Chapter 6.

The implications of varying epistemologies for teacher education are twofold. First, the kinds of epistemological beliefs that pre-service teachers hold affect the way they learn from their teacher education programmes (Hollingsworth, 1989;

Holt-Reynolds, 1992; Guilfoyle et al., 2020). Secondly, the kinds of epistemological beliefs that pre-service and in-service teachers hold affect the way they teach, and the ways that students learn from them (Brownlee et al., 2011; Maggioni & Parkinson, 2008). This affects not only students' learning of particular knowledge or subjects but also how they learn how to learn – explicit use of inquiry led learning, and strategies to support that increased students' self-directed learning competence in a study in Australian primary schools (Van Deur & Murray-Harvey, 2005).

Explanations

Explanations are the most prevalent discursive practice in most classrooms. Teachers explain new ideas or processes and procedures, connections between ideas, images, contexts and how to complete tasks and activities. Students can also explain to demonstrate their understanding of something, to persuade others, or to help them clarify their own thinking (Ingram et al., 2019). Explanations in classrooms are usually given for two reasons, to demonstrate understanding or to help someone else to understand (Donaldson, 1986). In primary science students' explanations might be more narrative initially and develop towards using scientific paradigms as part of their justification; teachers may model one more than the other depending on their beliefs about primary students' ability to handle abstract versus concrete thought (Peterson & French, 2008). Although making the point in the context of the primary school, this approach towards learning about and explaining new knowledge may move through a similar pattern at any phases of education: teachers (and students) continue moving between abstract and concrete modes of thought.

In mathematics, there is often a distinction between explanations that describe procedures or how to do something, and those that describe actions on mathematical objects and deal with the question of *why* (Perry, 2000; Yackel & Cobb, 1996).

Within these distinctions we also see debates around the role of proof and argumentation in mathematics, as students are more likely to accept proofs that explain (e.g. Healy & Hoyles, 2000; Sinclair et al., 2009). This leads to a contention in that proofs are often seen and treated as absolute verifications of the truth (or not) of something, and this is the main way they are presented within school mathematics. But in practice the acceptance of a proof is more subjective, which is highlighted in debates about whether visual proofs are in fact proofs at all! For example, Figure 1 illustrates that the sum of the first six odd numbers (1, 3, 5, 7, 9, 11) is a square number (6 squared or 36). However, by focusing on the structure of this image it is also illustrating that this will be true for the first n odd numbers (1, 3, 5, . . ., 2n-1) where their sum would be n^2. This

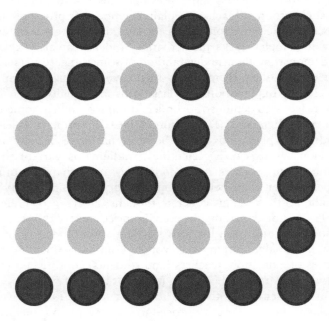

FIGURE 1 *The sum of a sequence of the consecutive odd numbers is a square number.*

image offers an explanation for *why* this relationship exists between odd numbers and square numbers which may not be apparent from the algebraic expression of the relationship that states *that* $\sum_{k=1}^{n} 2k - 1 = n^2$. More recently this debate has been extended by the use of computers and complex algorithms to generate proofs. This usually involves asking computers to check millions of cases until all possible types of case have been considered – proof by exhaustion – something that would take a human longer than their lifespan to do. But is this a proof if we cannot check the 'correctness' of each step? Is it the computer that is doing the proving, or is it just doing the calculations?

These epistemological distinctions within mathematics are not necessarily reflected in mathematics classrooms. Here, what matters is what is treated by teachers as being an explanation, or not, which can vary between classrooms (Ingram et al., 2019; Ingram & Andrews, 2020). Mathematics teachers often ask *why* questions, but in many instances students explaining how they calculated an answer is accepted as an answer to this *why* question – in other words, the distinction between *why* and *how* is obscured.

Explanation in English is likely to focus on the justification of an idea or interpretation, drawing on textual detail (or on a picture in early literacy), analogy with something else or personal experience. Through the dominance of essay-writing scaffolds like Point-Evidence-Explanation (Gibbons, 2019), explanation has become almost synonymous with detailed linguistic textual analysis in some cases. The explanation might be *why* the student thinks something, but it might equally be *how* the author has created an effect. In this way the explanation – the justification of the interpretation – becomes a key part of the construction of knowledge in English education. Similarly, historical explanation is seen as a core part of teaching and learning history (Van Drie & Van Boxtel, 2008; Seixas & Morton, 2013), and it is important that those historical explanations show historical causal relationships as complex and multifaceted (Lee & Shemilt, 2009). One challenge for history teachers is that students can come to see historical explanations as suggesting that historical outcomes were inevitable – predetermined – which leads to the strategy of engaging counterfactuals ('what ifs') in the classroom to qualify and support historical explanation (Wendell, 2020), a strategy that can be applied well in other subjects.

Explanation in geography includes a range of approaches spanning the natural and social sciences and humanities, as briefly described earlier through the distinctions between physical and human geography. However, explanation in school geography has received limited research attention, and so we know far less about it than in some other subject areas (particularly in comparison to mathematics and science education). This variation in research attention has implications for how we might speak across subjects, and a number of these points are raised throughout our discussions in this book. Chapter 6 – consequences for practice – brings some of these areas together to set an agenda for interdisciplinary research exploring questions about knowledge in teacher education further and in ways that draw on a rich diversity of traditions and perspectives.

One tension in geographical explanations that has been suggested by research is between empirical and perceptual accounts and abstract reasoning. Part of this tension comes through in Ruth's discussion: coming to know by 'actually seeing' and physically standing on a Drumlin, as opposed to the supposedly more tenuous process of analysing texts and making inferences. In the classroom, using images, photographs and videos mediates and represents these environments and processes, and there are important research questions to explore further about the relationships between these kinds of representational practices, students' understandings about geography and the ways in which they reason and construct explanations themselves. There is a great deal of tacit knowledge that students are expected to use in order to decide what counts as an appropriate explanation in each particular context, with variation within and between subjects.

An example from physical geography (discussed further in Chapter 3) draws on fieldwork experiences in limestone coastal environments, and the pedagogical dilemma about whether to tell students information about the rock types and landforms, or to enable the students to experience the processes through which geographers might come to know this information for themselves. This example generates interesting discussions that point to the complexity of what might initially be understood simply as 'actually seeing'. Mixing metaphors across landscapes, journeys and eating, Trudgill and Roy's (2003) discussion of 'meaning' in physical geography evokes the layered richness of knowledge as something with history:

> It is fundamentally important [to] recognize and understand the waypoint markers that have been passed in fashioning the sub-discipline. Knowledge, like landscape, in polygenetic, and whilst physical geographers 'graze' and hopefully absorb some of the nutrients from cognate disciplines, the 'foodstuff' needs to be fit for the purpose intended. Discussion on that fitness can only be informed by an acquaintance with what has gone before. (Trudgill & Roy, 2003, p. 17)

The educational aim – and the ways in which knowledge is understood and engaged with – drives the pedagogical choice of what kinds of explanations to use. There are complex subject-specific approaches towards generating knowledge which in part shape (or, maybe, *should* shape) teachers' explanations. Explanations seems to be an area that mentors frequently comment on in their lesson observation feedback to beginning teachers of geography (Puttick & Warren-Lee, 2021), and across subjects.

Understanding more about how explanations work in and between different subject areas, the relationships between these different kinds of explanations, and how initial teacher education might explore the ways in which mentors analyse and give feedback on beginning teachers' explanations are all important areas for research to address.

What Is the Nature of Knowledge

Within each discipline there are ways in which knowledge is established and accepted, as well as discipline-specific activities that 'experts' engage in. The relationships between these practices and those that are taught and enacted in classrooms are complex. Many curricula around the world explicitly reference some of these practices, such as problem solving in mathematics, enquiry and fieldwork in geography (Seow et al., 2020), nature of science in science education (Mork et al., 2022) and reasoning about sources in history (Pickles, 2011).

Geographical enquiry as a pedagogical approach has been developed in part to model the ways in which geographers see, understand and come to know the world. This approach to teaching geography is often described as being question-driven. In many cases this means that at the beginning of a lesson teachers make public the focus of the knowledge not by stating it explicitly, but through a question. These questions are designed to stimulate students' imagination, which might be done by reframing a statement about the knowledge to be taught into a question, for example: Through what processes is the coastline being shaped? What factors are increasing the flood risk? Others make the area of knowledge more implicit by presenting a (hopefully intriguing!) question, for example: Why are Sam's feet wet? and 'Why is Mrs Wilson having to replace her precious gnome collection' (Geographical Association, 2017)?

Similar developments are seen within mathematics teaching drawing on the habits of mind mathematicians engage in (Cuoco et al., 1996), the process of mathematical inquiry (*Inquiry Maths*, n.d.) and the processes of problem solving (Mason et al., 2010; Schoenfeld, 1985). The focus in each of these is in the actions and behaviours around a task or prompt. These behaviours include asking questions, looking for structures and patterns, working systematically, generalizing and abstracting, and convincing, justifying and proving. These are all activities that research mathematicians engage in. The challenge in mathematics teaching is not only for teachers to model these activities in their teaching but also of supporting students themselves to engage with these activities in meaningful or authentic ways (Ingram, 2021; Ingram & Riser, 2019).

In literary study we have mentioned already the core pedagogical approaches of shared reading and class discussion (Elliott, 2020). These reflect the ways in which experts construct knowledge – interpretations of texts – as well, although the interaction is more likely to be via the form of writing, with the thoughts of other experts.

All subjects to some extent suffer the problem of 'common sense' views of knowledge, the public view which is often promulgated by the media, held by parents and beloved of politicians. In English this 'common sense' tends to apply to the text choice, the importance of spelling or a particular interpretation of a text ('of course *Animal Farm* is about the Russian Revolution!'). Teachers often have to combat pushback from parents (and others) when the common sense test is breached, as in physics when light is both a particle and a wave, or the question of infinity in mathematics.

Shared Knowledge in the Classroom

The central aim of teaching and learning is that teachers and students come to share knowledge that is in focus. In a lesson on solving simple linear equations, by the end of the lesson the aim is that students will share sufficient knowledge with the teacher about how to solve particular equations. A literacy lesson might have the aim of generating a shared knowledge of the conventions of a particular genre of writing like the fairy

tale or the ghost story. A geography lesson might be planned
to generate a shared knowledge about the arguments for and
against the proposed location of a wind farm.

There are many activities and classroom practices that
teachers use to establish this shared knowledge at different
stages of a lesson or series of lessons. At the beginning of a
lesson many teachers include activities to establish or make
public the shared prior knowledge that the lesson is going to
build on. Lessons may be concluded with activities identifying
or summarizing 'what we learnt today'.

The centrality of shared knowledge is also implicit in the
types of interactions between teachers and students in lessons.
There has been research in mathematics education illustrating
a contrast in the way that students' saying that they 'don't
know' or that they 'don't remember' is treated differently by
teachers because of the way these phrases challenge or support
the assumption of knowledge being shared. When teachers ask
questions they often know the answer to these questions and
are expecting students to be able to answer these questions,
that is, that the knowledge needed for this question is shared.
When students respond that they don't remember, they are
taking responsibility and treating the knowledge as shared;
they just don't remember it. In response, teachers usually
redirect the question to a different student who may remember.
In contrast, when students' respond to say they 'don't know',
they are challenging the notion that the knowledge is shared.
In these situations, teachers usually persevere with the question
until the student gives an appropriate answer, possibly
simplifying the question or hinting to enable the student to
answer (Ingram, 2020).

Knowledge for the Real World

We end this chapter by considering the relationships between
knowledge in school and knowledge in pupils' everyday lives.
To what extent does the knowledge pupils need for their

examinations prepare them for the knowledge they will need in their everyday lives, both now and in the future?

PISA, an international large-scale assessment of reading, mathematical and scientific literacy, focuses specifically on whether students can use their knowledge and skills learnt in school to meet real-life challenges, across a range of contexts (OECD, n.d.). In their frameworks for the different subjects, OECD make distinctions between different knowledge types. For scientific literacy there is content, procedural and epistemic knowledge. For mathematical literacy the distinction is made between content knowledge and mathematical reasoning. For reading literacy, the distinction is between texts and processes. The results of these assessments influence educational policy across many countries, being used to argue that national performance needs to improve and to drive change (Breakspear, 2014).

Assessment as a way of thinking about what counts as knowledge in different disciplines – assessment validates knowledge. But we cannot measure all knowledge! And we cannot always measure things that are valued within a discipline. However, what gets measured is often what counts in school (Baird & Elliott, 2018). But is that the best way to judge what knowledge for the real world, as opposed to knowledge for school success, is required? In the next chapter we examine some of the key concepts in these debates further (particularly knowledge, skills and information). Chapter 3 then critically analyses one model – powerful knowledge – that seeks to define real-world value. There are also continuing debates over what knowledge schools should teach in relation to life skills – sex education, relationships education, financial education, careers education and so on. Situating these topics on the sidelines of school subjects, around the edges of the disciplinary knowledge, speaks to the value ascribed to them.

CHAPTER 3

Knowledge, Skills, Information and Technology

In this chapter we address the terminology of knowledge, information, skills and understanding, and the debates about their relative priority in education. We consider the ways in which 'knowledge' functions discursively in these debates, and in particular the constructed dichotomy between knowledge and skills, and how that relates to beliefs about the purpose of education, such as rhetorical links to social mobility via a certain conception of cultural capital, or a focus on the preparation of students for future employment.

Core Knowledge or Cultural Capital?

One ongoing debate is whether education should focus on teaching knowledge versus teaching skills. There has been what might be described as a 'knowledge turn' in education over the last few years, which has focused on the importance of knowledge as a tool in closing attainment gaps and for improving social mobility. This is tied up in the 'powerful knowledge' question, which is explored further in Chapter 5, but in addition, in the United States has been focused around E. D. Hirsch's 'cultural literacy' (1987) and the subsequent 'core knowledge' curricula which have been developed around this model. In the UK this debate has focused instead on 'cultural capital', although the ways in which this term is used by government and in teaching has far more to do with the Hirschean cultural literacy than with Pierre Bourdieu's original conception of cultural capital. Exponents of cultural literacy and cultural capital as the basis of systematized teaching both claim the social justice moral high ground, in that they argue that learning particular sets of knowledge is essential for educational, and therefore later life, success. One exam board in the UK issued training materials including the line 'Whilst schools can do little to improve a student's immediate socio-economic situation, we can increase social mobility if we improve their cultural capital' (AQA, 2018, p. 8).

To take cultural literacy first. To be culturally literate is to have the level of background knowledge that enables you to partake in the national social discourse; defined by Hirsch as 'the background information, stored in [readers'] minds, that enables them to take up a newspaper and read it with an adequate level of comprehension, getting the point, grasping the implications, relating what they read to the unstated context which alone gives meaning to what they read' (Hirsch, 1987, p. 2). A detailed level of knowledge is not required; this is the kind of general knowledge that enables someone to understand allusions to a wide range of references while reading. They would recognize 'a curse on both your houses' as being from *Romeo and Juliet* but they would not necessarily have studied the play.

The required knowledge to be culturally literate varies by country. Hirsch includes, for example, important landmarks in his list of examples. His original list, which is constructed by reference to the United States, includes Mount Vernon. Mount Vernon was George Washington's plantation home, and the only context you are likely to find it in outside the United States is in the film *National Treasure 2: Book of Secrets.*

The British equivalent might be to know what Chequers (the prime minister's country home) is, but again it is not a piece of knowledge which is necessary for cultural literacy in other English-speaking countries. In Australia knowing of Uluru would be essential; most other English-speaking countries would provide a gloss when referring to it or use the name Ayers Rock. Elliott has argued that 'Cultural literacy is a thin veneer of knowledge which enables understanding references in the wider discourse without requiring in-depth knowledge' (Elliott, 2020, p. 102).

Any official list of essential items for cultural literacy raises the question of who gets to choose what goes on that list. Hirsch's original list (1987) was created by him (a literary critic) in collaboration with a historian and a physicist, then finalized with feedback from 100 other experts. These 100 were largely white, male and middle-class. However, even with the 5,000 items on his list, he noted that 'No such compilation can be definitive . . . different literate Americans have slightly different conceptions of our shared knowledge. The authors see the list as a changing entity, partly because core knowledge changes, partly because inappropriate omissions and inclusions are bound to occur in a first attempt' (Hirsch, 1987, p. 146).

Here the terms 'core knowledge' and 'shared knowledge' are used, rather than cultural literacy, which removes the emphasis from 'culture' which has been one of the prime causes of confusion over cultural capital in the UK. In a Bourdieuan sense, cultural capital is the capital (on a model from economic or human capital) that accrues from being part of a specific culture and enables you to move within the group associated with that culture. The culture is not necessarily 'high' culture (e.g. opera, literary fiction, classical art).

> Bourdieu's concept of cultural capital refers to the collection of symbolic elements such as skills, tastes, posture, clothing, mannerisms, material belongings, credentials, etc. that one acquires through being part of a particular social class. Sharing similar forms of cultural capital with others – the

same taste in movies, for example, or a degree from an Ivy League School – creates a sense of collective identity and group position ('people like us'). But Bourdieu also points out that cultural capital is a major source of social inequality. Certain forms of cultural capital are valued over others, and can help or hinder one's social mobility just as much as income or wealth. (Cultural Capital | Social Theory Rewired, n.d.)

It is not the accumulation of cultural capital itself which contributes to social inequality, but that certain forms of cultural capital are considered to be more valuable than others, by the people who arbitrate educational examinations, curriculum and even school standards. The English schools inspectorate Ofsted explicitly now makes judgements on this when visiting schools:

As part of making the judgement about quality of education, inspectors will consider the extent to which schools are equipping pupils with the knowledge and cultural capital they need to succeed in life. Ofsted's understanding of this knowledge and cultural capital matches the understanding set out in the aims of the national curriculum. It is the essential knowledge that pupils need to be educated citizens, introducing them to the best that has been thought and said, and helping to engender an appreciation of human creativity and achievement. (Ofsted, 2019, p. 10)

The framing of cultural capital in these contexts is very definitely as knowledge of high culture and largely revolves around the use of classical literature and music in curricula, visiting museums and theatres, and history that revolves around monarchs and dates, as well as potentially learning Latin and Greek, or even using the right cutlery and a table cloth.

Knowledge versus Skills

Both cultural capital and cultural literacy – and powerful knowledge – frame knowledge as being key to social mobility, or eliminating the gaps in outcomes that arise from social inequality. In particular there has been a tendency in 'edutwitter' to frame knowledge in opposition to skills, and to frame the rote learning of information as being key to life success for students. 'Knowledge-rich' is a term which is particularly popular in describing curricula. 'Knowledge' in public debates over education has been discursively framed as being the domain of 'trads' (traditional teachers) as opposed to 'progs' (progressive teachers) with an implication that these are also on the spectrum of conservative to socialist politics. In doing so knowledge has formed part of the discursive reclamation by the right of social justice and social mobility from the left. This debate has constructed a strawman that prior to the last few years and the rise of cognitive science in education (see later) schools and teachers were letting students down by concentrating on skills over knowledge. In framing this opposition the discourse means we rarely talk of 'understanding' as a key aim of learning any more, although it remains an important aspect of how knowledge can be put to work.

In truth there has always been a combination of both knowledge and skills (and indeed understanding!) in the curriculum. An example of a geography fieldtrip to a Mediterranean limestone coast presents a dilemma facing the teacher: in this context is it more important for the students to know the answer, or to know about and to experience the process through which subject specialists come to know the answer? The example illustrates something of the combination of knowledge, skills and understanding that permeate classrooms (and particularly in the case, teaching situations outside classrooms!). The teacher – Trudgill (2003) – asked the students to look at the coastal limestone landforms in Mallorca that they were standing on and which surrounded them, and then to describe and explain them to him. What he 'saw' and what his students 'saw' were quite different things: 'the limestone rocks were dissected and rugged and, to [Trudgill's] mind, etched by biochemical processes involving boring algae and salt weathering', whereas the students 'came back with descriptive words like "lunar" and they asked if it was not obviously volcanic lava' (Trudgill, 2003, p. 27). Faced with this kind of dilemma, what should the teacher do? What is the most *geographical* approach? How should teacher educators equip teachers to explain geographical knowledge? Trudgill's description gives some insight into the reasoning through which he made he pedagogical decisions:

> The students were not equipped to come up with the 'right answer' and were using the only constructs they had in their mind, in a clearly comparative sense – 'it looks like . . .' – something else they already had knowledge of. If they had looked long enough and used hand lenses, eventually they would have discovered the minute pitting which the boring algae leave and, using an acid bottle, they would come up with limestone rather than volcanic rock and so on. But to me this illustrated a general theme: our explanations refer to what we already know, and when presented with the unknown we readily refer to our existing constructs, partly because that is the obvious thing to do and partly as it excuses us somewhat from the effort of trying to see what is actually there. But what, in fact, is actually there? . . . My task was to point out features inconsistent with their explanations, but still the task is to get the students to observe – to actually see – rather than to rest on their preconceptions. (p.27)

The dilemma sparks many different possible responses, and there is much that we might discuss about the pedagogical approach, the situation it makes possible and the ways in which teachers might manage these kinds of dilemmas. We are particularly interested in the way in which the nature of geography is represented through this example as a fundamentally experiential and empirical discipline: the aim driving the choice of explanations to use is to empower students that they might 'actually see'. This is subtly – but significantly – different to 'knowing the right answer' being the aim driving the choice of explanations to use. Instead, there are subject-specific concerns about introducing students to geography itself, enabling them to become familiar with doing geography rather than just knowing things about geography.

Do you need knowledge before you can learn a skill? To learn to write, you need to have something to write about. But that something is more likely to come from what Vygotsky labelled 'everyday knowledge' (or 'spontaenous concepts') rather than the school learned 'scientific knowledge' (e.g. see discussion of the distinction between Vygotsky's everyday and scientific knowledge in Daniels, 2015, p. 6). Wineburg argues that some issues have arisen from the treatment of Bloom's taxonomy as a hierarchy and as a prescriptive rather than descriptive tool: 'at its bottom lay *knowledge*. A precursor to the levels that came later, it formed a base from which students might ascend to steeper, more impressive heights' (Wineburg, 2018, p. 83). For him

the pyramid is upside down. Putting knowledge at the base implies that the world of ideas is fully known and that critical thinking means gathering accepted facts into order to render judgment. Bloom's pyramid endows knowledge with all the glamour of a dank basement: necessary for a house's foundation but hardly the place to host honored guests . . . . Of course knowledge is a prerequisite to critical thinking. At the same time, knowledge represents its highest aim. (Wineburg, 2018, p. 92)

Debates about knowledge can become deeply acrimonious in the education sphere, particularly where people are highly invested in their own beliefs and practices as being socially just, given the popular conception of teaching as a vocation.

Why Can't I Just Look It Up on My Phone?

Challenges to the importance of 'knowledge' come from the ubiquity of technology as children, and many adults, rely on the ability to simply google whatever they need to find out at any given moment.

One Platonic definition of knowledge is that it is 'justified true belief' – that is, that there are three components to knowing a thing – that that thing must be true, you must believe it and you must be justified in believing it, that is you must have a reason for doing so. Where the internet falls down is the first of these criteria, and Amoore (2020) returns to the question of 'truth' when it comes to the internet and the material which algorithms prioritize. But the third criteria, being justified in your belief, is also problematic, because of the ways in which we interact with and interpret the material we encounter via search engines.

The internet is supposed to have democratized information and knowledge, which in some ways it has, in enabling 'individuals to bypass traditional information portals, seen as encapsulating establishment networks of control, so as to become personally empowered to create, locate or upload content that is not reliant upon gatekeepers or tastemakers for validation and dispersal' (Gauld, 2017, p. 233). Access to digitalized archives, books, manuscripts, photographs and much more is increasing on a daily basis. The challenge for knowledge – for students and for teachers – is no longer in accessing information, but in knowing what sources to trust and how to evaluate those sources.

Wineburg (2018) describes a number of internet knowledge-finding experiments in which participants are hardly able to decipher why they clicked on one link rather than another, or assume that the higher up the search results the item comes, the more reliable the source. The function of algorithms in search engines drives the visibility (or non-visibility) of some information and knowledge in searches, reproducing and reinforcing real-world biases (Amoore, 2020; Noble, 2018). Herein lies the problem of replacing gatekeepers with data-driven freedom of access: one set of biases is replaced by another set which disguises itself as neutrality (Gauld, 2017). The internet is not neutral. Noble's *Algorithms of Oppression* (2018) provides a thorough discussion of the ways in which search engines reinforce racism, primarily because the algorithms replicate and intensify societal prejudices, because search engines reflect the interests of advertisers (which often means sellers of pornography), and because extremist individuals and organizations are adept at SEO (Search Engine Optimization) so that, for example, searching for Jewish history can lead you to Holocaust denial with alarming rapidity.

In another study historians – professional assessors of sources! – were unable to distinguish between the reliability of the American College of Pediatricians and the American Academy of Pediatrics, one of which is a large professional group with 64,000 members, and the other a breakaway group that opposes adoption by same sex couples (Wineburg, 2018). What hope do 13-year-olds Googling for their homework have?

As we have moved from an age of limited access to information to an age of information overload, there are several implications for both teachers and students. It is no longer about simply finding the relevant information but also about judging the reliability of the source of the information. This means that before setting 'research' homeworks teachers will need to teach twenty-first-century research skills. We have moved from 'check in the encyclopaedia' through 'don't just accept what Wikipedia says' to an age of deliberate and extensive 'fake news'.

Wineburg (2018, pp. 150–2) suggests 'lateral reading' as a productive strategy for reading and evaluating information on the internet. This is a technique by which, having discovered a page purporting to provide the information you need, you open another tab – or many other tabs – to check on its credentials and cross-check. You might first search for the name of the organization whose page your information is on; you might check it on Wikipedia but flick straight to the references at the bottom of the page and see what they say. (It is a weird fact of life that Wikipedia is now one of the most peer-reviewed sources on the internet.) When given a piece of information, you might then google that statement to see if it can be corroborated from other sources. This is a time-consuming activity just as much for teachers as for students. For teachers this may mean a greater reliance on other people's research skills, on pre-prepared curriculum resources (but whose can you trust?), or a need to utilize their disciplinary knowledge to evaluate what they have found. 'The internet has obliterated authority' (Wineburg, 2018, p. 3) allowing everyone to be an instant expert and to make claims for truth: inexperienced and experienced readers alike find it difficult to tell the difference.

One particularly key issue for educators in relation to the internet is the proliferation of 'fake news', and the mass dissemination of misinformation. Learning about how to identify evidence, to evaluate sources, to consider authorial intentions and to construct the most accurate picture – the best knowledge – possible, is a key tenet of a number of different school subjects, including history, geography, media, English. The term 'critical literacy' has become unfashionable to a certain extent (as a 'skill' rather than knowledge!) but it captures this needed scepticism to much of what our students are exposed to on the internet.

At the very cutting edge of questions about technology in education is the existence of ChatGPT and the proliferation of AI-generated text. Leaving aside concerns about plagiarism and the consequences for assessment which are outside the remit of our discussion, there are, according to ChatGPT itself,

'significant implications for knowledge in education. With its ability to understand and generate human-like responses to a wide range of questions and topics, it has the potential to revolutionize the way students learn and acquire knowledge. ChatGPT can provide students with personalized learning experiences, where they can ask questions and receive immediate and accurate answers, and it can also assist teachers in creating lesson plans and curricula that are tailored to the specific needs of their students. Additionally, ChatGPT's vast knowledge base can be used to augment and enhance traditional learning materials, such as textbooks and lectures, by providing real-time and interactive explanations and examples. Overall, ChatGPT has the potential to democratize access to knowledge and provide a more engaging and effective learning experience for students'. (ChatGPT in response to the prompt 'write a paragraph about the implications of ChatGPT for knowledge in education'.)

This is a wide-ranging set of ideas for how Generative AI may become embedded in our classrooms. There are implications for teacher education here too, as the idea of using AI-generated lesson plan or schemes of work for learning purposes – as models to unpick, or as starting points – could be a useful tool for beginning teachers. Interactive use of Generative AI in classroom situations, for the production of model answers to emulate, or to contrast with students' own answers to questions, could indeed provide an 'engaging and effective learning experience'.

Beyond this, unfortunately, we might not have such as positive view of ChatGPT as the AI has of itself. The tendency of ChatGPT to invent plausible sounding sources which do not in fact exist (King, 2023) makes it problematic in terms of use as knowledge in education. As with most technology the problems arise in its use rather than its existence, and AI chatbots will undoubtedly be a more prominent part of classrooms, whether in secret or in the open, in the years to come.

Cognitive Psychology

Cognitive science is becoming increasingly influential in pedagogy (Perry et al., 2021); a plethora of professional resources and books have appeared in recent years claiming to have the answer to how learning happens based on recent (and not so recent) developments in cognitive psychology and cognitive neuroscience. Perry et al.'s (2021) systematic review of the evidence concluded that while 'basic cognitive science and applied cognitive science have the potential to offer, respectively, significant insights into learning and pedagogic practice', 'the rapid popularisation of cognitive science inspired practice has led to the premature recommendation – and even mandating – of education practice underpinned by particular elements of cognitive science' (p. 264). They particularly warned about the cross-application of findings between subjects, age ranges and contexts when these were often quite dissimilar areas. In Chapter 2 we explored the ways in which different subjects may work differently in regards to knowledge: it stands to reason that the same ways of learning may not transfer across these subjects.

One very popular activity drawn from cognitive science is retrieval practice, in which testing knowledge – that is, asking students to retrieve it – helps to promote its transfer into long-term memory (Rowland, 2014). This is perhaps one of the most well-evidenced phenomena in learning science, and is well-embedded in classrooms across the globe. Many schools use retrieval practice in parallel with 'knowledge organizers', lists of key facts and information which students are required to learn during a unit of work. These then supply the material for teachers to design the quick quizzes which are used to provide the retrieval practice.

Utilizing this approach to retrieval practice without reducing knowledge down to memorizable facts is in fact quite difficult. It is easy to imagine the definition of a horse given by Bitzer to Mr Gradgrind's approval in Dickens' *Hard Times* would fit easily into such an organizer:

Quadruped. Graminivorous. Forty teeth, namely twenty-four grinders, four eye-teeth, and twelve incisive. Sheds coat in the spring; in marshy countries, sheds hoofs, too. Hoofs hard, but requiring to be shod with iron. Age known by marks in mouth. (Dickens, 1854/ 1986)

It may be 170 years since *Hard Times* was written, but it exemplifies perfectly the potential tensions around knowledge in the age of the cognitive turn – does this boy know what a horse is, or not? Does hearing this mean you know what a horse is, or not? In every subject there is some simple factual information whose learning by heart can be of use: times tables and equations in mathematics, some dates in history, locations of places in geography, definitions of terms, spellings and so on. But a heavy-handed commitment to the 'what works' of retrieval practice can lead to an emphasis on the kinds of knowledge which can be easily summarized, tested, 'retrieved'. A bias towards low-level factual knowledge results, rather than a deep engagement with disciplinary understanding and knowledge.

Knowledge versus Information

The question which has been consistently raised throughout this chapter is 'what is the difference between knowledge and information?' One suggested key distinction is that information exists independently of the human mind, but knowledge requires someone to 'know' it. Another is that information is organized data but that knowledge is that information put to use, interpreted or experienced and internalized. The fact that information has to be transformed in some way in order to become knowledge demonstrates the limits to the 'banking' model of education in which teachers 'deposit' information into the empty vessel that is a student's brain (Freire, 1968). Students have to be more than passive receptors in order to transform information which they are given into knowledge.

One of the key ways in which we turn information into knowledge is placing it into a context. Mental schemas are one way of conceptualizing this, a 'bundle of knowledge stored in memory' (Giovanelli & Mason, 2015, p. 45). The schema or 'bundle' is organized in such a way that we can connect new information to it and create an increase in our knowledge. Giovanelli and Mason use this concept to discuss knowledge of texts in English classrooms, but it applies across the range of disciplines. Learning dates out of context in history, for example, is hard, but individual dates which are connected to networks of knowledge about, for example the French Revolution, become embedded and useful. Thinking about this model may also help to inform the use of knowledge organizers (or are they really information organizers?) in the classroom.

Getting It Wrong – Mistakes, Errors and Misconceptions

One of the most important aspects of thinking about learning of knowledge in education is the ways in which students can get it wrong, and what happens when they do. It is in the literature on feedback that we find the most helpful material on this topic, and particularly in the fields of applied linguistics and computer-based instruction. Some of the literature makes a distinction between 'mistakes' – something a student can do, and does normally do, correctly, but has not on this occasion – and 'errors' which are something that a student has not mastered, or which are patterns of consistent errors. Mistakes should be easily correctable by students, so Bitchener and Ferris (2012) recommend identifying them but not correcting them. In the context of retrieval practice, where simple lower-level recall is required, giving students the correct answer is effective and aids learning (Morrison et al., 1995). In general giving hints to students about how they can correct their own mistake is more effective in creating cognitive engagement (Ferris, 2001), so that students think more carefully about how they came about.

When errors are 'treatable', that is students can self-correct them because they are rule-governed, then teachers can give hints, and let students work them out for themselves (Ferris, 2001). When students make errors which don't follow a rule or procedure, or ones which occur very often, or which are 'stigmatizing' (i.e. which would generate a negative reaction from other students, examiners or employers), teachers should correct those errors (Bitchener & Ferris, 2012). This idea of stigma links back to the questions of cultural capital and cultural literacy, and particularly ideas around correct language. A stigmatizing error is most likely to relate to basic literacy and numeracy knowledge.

The idea of stigma around mistakes is interesting and is deeply connected to some of the research in mathematics education around the ways in which errors and mistakes are treated in the classroom. Some researchers have promoted the idea of using errors as opportunities for learning, while others have noted the potential for embarrassment on the part of the student, depending on the classroom climate (Bray, 2011). Although the predominant advice has shifted to using errors as learning moments, Ingram et al.'s (2015) research on whole-class interactions in mathematics classrooms uses a conversation analytic approach to demonstrate that teachers still treat mistakes as 'dispreferred' and avoid giving direct negative evaluations to students. This gives the idea to students that mistakes are to be avoided, which can lead to a reluctance to attempt answering when they are not sure. Although this is in a single subject, how teachers conversationally treat errors or mistakes is something to think about in relation to other school subjects, and indeed in teacher education seminars.

In some cases errors are the result of misconceptions. Misconception is a term which has been most clearly defined in the literature on science and mathematics learning. In these contexts misconceptions arise from intuitive understandings; as young children learn more 'they develop new and revised concepts based on their interpretation of this new information from the viewpoint of their existing ideas and beliefs' (Canpolat et al., 2006, p. 1237). This is analogous to the idea of mental schema discussed earlier. If the concepts students develop are not consistent with accepted scientific consensus they are misconceptions. Errors that result from misconceptions make sense to learners because they develop out of their other knowledge. Therefore, misconceptions cannot be simply 'removed' or 'replaced' by teachers but rather need to be 'restructured' by the learners themselves (Smith III et al., 1994). This requirement for learners to restructure their thinking has led to a concentration of research on task design which can generate 'cognitive conflict' with the aim of exposing students' misconceptions to the students themselves (Bray, 2013; Swan, 2008; Zaslavsky, 2005). Gil-Perez and Carrascosa (1990) suggested that science learning could be seen as being primarily concerned with conceptual change. This also has implications for what the nature of knowledge is: it is not only about facts and concrete information but also about the more abstract and harder to grasp concepts which underlie the way we understand the world.

Childs and Wong (forthcoming) pick up on the idea of conceptual change in relation to the models which are offered in science learning. As students progress through secondary school they are offered progressively more complex models to explain phenomena; they are often told with each new model that the previous model was wrong. Childs and Wong challenge this on the grounds that it is both demotivating and that as teacher educators they 'have come across many adults, including science graduates, who were similarly put off chemistry by being told to forget what they had learnt in previous years as it was wrong' (forthcoming). They suggest instead that it should be emphasized that models are chosen to help explain the necessary concepts '*at that level* and that, as concepts become more demanding, different models are needed' (forthcoming). The example that Childs and Wong use is the model of what an atom is; a more complex version is produced for different levels of student. The model at each level is considered to be knowledge. This idea that knowledge is not fixed but subject to change (as expressed in the quotation from Wineburg (2018)) is returned to across the chapters that follow. We have highlighted some of the significant ways in which these changes are happening in relation to technology. Discussions around (and policy responses to) technological advances are becoming increasingly important as the rate of change continues to increase, as the tools become more accessible to more people and as the aims and purposes of education evolve in response to our changing world. These debates continue in the chapters that follow, particularly when considering the relationships between knowledge and power (Chapter 5) and the challenges involved with pursuing knowledge for all (Chapter 6).

CHAPTER 4

Teacher Knowledge

What knowledge do teachers need? What types of knowledge are most important for teaching? In what ways is teacher knowledge distinctive? How do teachers gain the knowledge they need? Teacher knowledge has been widely debated both within research and policy for over fifty years. The early ideas that teachers who *know* more will demonstrate better teaching have long been challenged and refuted, but this assumption has led to arguments around what teachers 'need to know', what makes a good teacher, and even the nature of teaching itself.

In research, the notion of pedagogical content knowledge (PCK) has captured much interest and enthusiasm over the years. Shulman (1986) initially proposed PCK as the special combination of subject content and pedagogy that positions teacher knowledge as a type of knowledge that is specific and unique to the discipline of teaching. These arguments about the distinctive knowledge held by teachers fed into debates about whether teaching was a profession like law and medicine, rather than being ('only') a technical job. The historical and social contexts in which these discussions have happened also intersect with gendered and other inequalities:

> Teaching is largely feminized, while no traditional profession is. The handiest parallel to teaching from this standpoint is nursing, which suffers from the same relatively low status, low pay, and subjection to (generally male) administrative

authority that teaching does. Our society's tendency to undervalue 'women's work' constitutes a major impediment to the attainment of professional status by teachers. (Burbules & Densmore, 1991)

Written in the United States over thirty years ago, these discourses continue to reflect some of the contemporary issues surrounding the status of teaching as a profession, although there are marked differences in teachers' status internationally. In particular, between the relatively high professional status (and public perception of this status) in Finland against the relatively lower status and perceptions of teacher status in the UK (Rinne & Ozga, 2020). These differences in status are despite the fact that the distinctiveness of teachers' knowledge – in Shulman's terms, their PCK – and the expectations on their expertise have great similarities across the countries.

In the years that have followed Shulman's work, research has focused on identifying, measuring and supporting the development of this knowledge that teachers need to be effective in their practice. Yet this notion of knowledge as something teachers have has also been challenged, with many arguing that it is knowing what to do, when and why in the moment in the act of teaching that marks teacher knowledge (or knowing!) as something special and specific. This is a shift from focusing on what teachers know to how teachers' knowing comes into being.

This chapter explores a range of perspectives and considers what knowledges teachers need, the nature of this knowledge and how teachers can develop that knowledge, by addressing questions such as what does it mean for teachers to know-that, know-how, know-why and know-to? The different conceptions of teacher knowledge or knowing, drawing from a range of theoretical perspectives, reveal the complexity of finding answers to these questions. This complexity is compounded by similarities and differences between discipline-specific conceptions which we considered in Chapter 2, and the relationship between theory and practice which prepares the way for the discussions in Chapter 6 (*Knowledge for All*).

The Components of Teacher Knowledge

What knowledge do teachers need? This question has been of interest to researchers, teacher educators and policymakers for many years, but for different reasons and in different ways. The answers offered for this question are also highly contested, depending upon the conceptions of teacher learning; the goals, values and purposes of schooling and education; and the role of teachers within these. In a growing number of contexts, teachers' knowledge is assessed in a variety of ways as part of their initial teacher education course, or as part of teacher accountability measures and evaluation systems.

It is widely argued that teachers need more than expertise in the subject area(s) that they are teaching or specific skills in classroom management, and Shulman's (1986) captured this idea in the notion of PCK. He describes PCK as including 'the most regularly taught topics in one's subject area, the most useful forms of representation of those ideas, the most powerful analogies, illustrations, examples, explanations, and demonstrations' (p. 9). There are now a range of models and frameworks of PCK, and research in this area has been and continues to be extensive: some of this work is focused on particular subject areas, such as Hume et al. (2019) in science, Backman and Barker (2020) in physical education and Schiener et al. (2019) in mathematics; other research incorporates the use of technologies or assessments or curricula (e.g., Schmid et al. (2020) or Khoza and Biyela (2020)), and others that offer different perspectives on the nature of this knowledge (Copur-Gencturk et al., 2019). For many researchers PCK, and knowledge more generally, is relatively stable or static and there is a focus on measuring and listing this knowledge. In some contexts, this measuring of teacher knowledge has resulted in teachers needing to pass tests to qualify, or gain employment, and in much research has led to teachers being labelled as 'good' if they meet a particular threshold on their measures of teacher knowledge (Guerriero, 2017).

These approaches to teacher knowledge often focus on specific aspects such as knowledge of students' common difficulties or appropriate analogies or representations, that is, the parts of PCK. Yet Settlage (2013) critiqued this work on PCK, both challenging the idea of teacher knowledge as being 'store[d] in their heads' (p. 10) and calling for more evidence of a relationship between these different measures of PCK and the impact of teaching on students' learning. Borowski and colleagues (2012) further problematize the use of PCK in research, illustrating the different ways that researchers have conceptualized PCK and the relationship between knowledge and practice.

While for researchers PCK is difficult to articulate and conceptualize (Lee & Luft, 2008), for teacher educators the notion is often useful in framing the learning of teachers, as well as in offering an explanation for why strong content knowledge and classroom management is not sufficient for effective teaching. This role of PCK is also reflected in teacher education research where knowing and understanding are active processes (Cochran et al., 1993), where teacher knowledge is more than the sum of its parts and there is a focus on developing teachers' knowing and understanding as well as studying teachers' decision making in practice. Here the attention is on what teacher knowledge, including PCK, might look like in action. PCK focuses on what distinguishes teachers' subject disciplinary knowledge from that of academics. Knowledge for teaching (KfT) on the other hand focuses on the distinctions between subjects, such as the differences between teaching mathematics, English or geography. Each of these foci offers different insights into what makes teaching a particular subject distinctive and specialized.

At the core of debates around pedagogical content knowledge is an interest in how teachers transform their subject content in ways that make it comprehensible for their students. This transformation occurs not only during the planning and preparation of teaching (Fargher et al., 2021) but also through contingent moments within the classroom (Rowland et al., 2005). A dynamic view of this transformation has also contributed to distinctions between knowing-that, knowing-how and knowing-why that focus on the forms of knowing that are being taught, and knowing-to act in the moment in the classroom (Adoniou, 2015; Mason & Spence, 1999). PCK is both idiosyncratic and dependent upon the topic that is being taught. It is also developed over time and can be influenced by a range of educational and pedagogical experiences (i.e. both through continuing professional development and through time in the classroom). The influence of practice on PCK was formulated by Grimmet and MacKinnon (1992) as 'craft knowledge', although this has been misinterpreted and oversimplified to support on-the-job apprenticeships and learning by doing models as sufficient teacher preparation (Olsen, 2014). We would advocate, along with many others, the need for theoretical and empirical knowledge, as well as reflection on practice as an essential part of developing knowledge for teaching (whether that be PCK or another formulation).

Alongside PCK, many models of the knowledge that teachers need also include content knowledge (including substantive structures and syntactic structures of an academic discipline), curricula knowledge, knowledge of students, knowledge of assessment, knowledge at the subject horizon. Yet distinctions between these categories are difficult to make, with many arguing that content knowledge is inherently pedagogical for example. Further, beliefs and orientations around subjects, and the purpose or goals of schools and teaching in relation to these subjects, are often tightly connected to knowledge or knowing. These influences and interconnections are considered in a variety of ways, for example Gess-Newsome (2015) describes these beliefs and orientations as amplifiers and filters that mediate how teachers act and learn. We will return to these influences later in the discussion around teacher learning, where beliefs, attitudes and goals are integral to many models of teacher learning and growth.

So, each of these perspectives on teacher knowledge argue that teachers need to know more than the subject matter that they teach, and they need to know this in a different way from experts in the subject matter. Furthermore, teachers also need to know how to structure or organize this subject matter in ways that enable their students to gain this knowledge themselves.

Teacher Knowledge as Action or Interaction

Another way of looking at teacher knowledge is to focus on teacher actions; on the decisions teachers make or need to make in the classroom, and to understand this as an evolving process. Here it is the interaction between knowledge, the teacher and the classroom context that is in focus. This also requires a shift from thinking about how teachers transform knowledge for their students to thinking about the interactions between students and the subject matter (Scheiner et al., 2019). For some, this is knowledge-in-action. For others, there is an underlying premise that teacher knowledge is situated and cultural, and not something that resides in an individual teacher's head. The development of teacher knowledge is also contextual and social; the knowledge that teachers develop is jointly constituted by their actions and the context in which they act. The active nature of this knowledge leads to some preferring the term 'teacher knowing' to 'teacher knowledge'. The interactional nature from some perspectives also highlights the relationship between teacher knowledge and student knowledge, for example, from an interactionist or discursive psychology perspective teacher knowledge may be associated with interactional constructions of pupils as not knowledgeable (Barwell, 2013).

This teacher knowledge is also largely tacit and implicit, which has also contributed to the use of observational methods that have dominated the research into teacher knowledge that takes these perspectives. Many of these methods and perspectives have emphasized how teacher knowledge is dynamic and fluid, co-constructed through interaction, as well as being context specific. It is not something that can be identified or measured by talking to teachers or by teachers completing questionnaires. This situated view focuses on the details of classroom practice and interactions between teachers, students and subject matter. This means that the teacher knowledge observed in one lesson will be different from the teacher knowledge observed in another even where the teacher, content and class are the same.

While this view of teacher knowledge poses many challenges to researchers and policymakers, it often resonates with the lived experiences of teachers and teacher educators. It also highlights the contingent nature of teaching, where teachers have to make multiple decisions in very short periods of time where there is no clear 'right' action to take. These actions require teachers to balance multiple demands and goals simultaneously.

Knowledge at the Horizon

In the next chapter we begin to explore the similarities and differences between subject knowledge and disciplinary knowledge in a range of curriculum areas. These distinctions are particularly relevant to our discussions of the question: What knowledge do teachers need to know? Knowledge at the horizon refers to the knowledge that teachers need that is beyond the school curriculum. This could be unifying concepts or themes that run through the school curriculum but are not necessarily explicit in the curriculum (Watson, 2008; Zazkis & Mamolo, 2011). It could also be more advanced content that the knowledge in school is foundational to, that may influence both what and how different concepts or ideas are taught in school. Or it could be particular, discipline-specific ways of behaving, thinking, or working, for example, acting like a mathematician, geographer or a poet.

In mathematics an example of this knowledge can be illustrated in the distinction between inverses and reciprocals. Students are introduced to the notation for the inverse of a function after they have met the same notation but in the context of indices where it refers to the reciprocal of a term. Teachers need to draw upon their understanding of functions and inverses within group theory that are with respect to a particular operation to understand the distinction being made, but they would not make this knowledge at the horizon explicit in their explanations to students (Zazkis & Mamolo, 2011).

In geography, teachers often draw on current events in the news to illustrate the more theoretical concepts and processes that they have been teaching about. The recency of these events means that they are not in the curriculum, nor are they in the textbook. Teachers need to draw upon their understanding of the concepts and processes (and their critical media literacy) in order to interpret and apply this new information. Their knowledge at the horizon is in this case looking beyond the curriculum to see how these events can be geographically understood. Among many questions, teachers might ask at the horizon: Do these concepts still apply? In what ways might these concepts offer insights into how we understand the events? How do these new situations challenge and refine our previous understandings? What are the similarities and differences with previous cases? Who is being represented, and in what ways? What are the implications of these representations? At what temporal and spatial scales might this be best understood? What connections between this event and other people, things, places and processes should we foreground and explore further?

In literature, the knowledge at the horizon can be almost endless: intertextuality means that all texts are essentially in conversation with one another, with overlapping layers of influence and allusion taking place. Sawyer and McLean Davies argue that there is 'no sufficient answer' to the question 'what knowledge' is relevant for study for any particular text (2021, p. 106). It is simply not possible for one teacher to have all of the right textual details and knowledge in order to address any given text (which gives an added air of uncertainty to the question of authoritative knowledge in literature!). Student questions and interpretations push this horizon further away from what can be pre-planned: in any given Shakespeare play the number of references, innovations, plays on words, metaphors, similes, descriptions or vocabulary form a cloud of potentially relevant items that could be pulled back from the horizon and brought into sharp focus. Not only that but the kinds of knowing which are brought into being in the English classroom go far beyond disciplinary, literary or historical knowledge, as students are able to use not only their own experience to understand texts but also texts to understand their own experience (e.g. McLean Davies et al., 2023).

Developing Teacher Knowledge

Another fundamental question is how teachers learn and develop the knowledge they need. Classrooms are complex and dynamic spaces that teachers need to manage, and adapt and respond to, in order to achieve a range of (learning) goals. Throughout their careers teachers will experience a diverse range of students, curricula and technological developments. This complexity and fluidity means that the knowledge teachers need 'is continuously changing, updating, refocussing and recontextualising' (Santoro et al., 2013, p. 125).

There are a range of models and theories of teacher learning and growth, not only during initial teacher education but also extending beyond to teacher professional development. It is now widely recognized that teacher learning is complex, dynamic, contextual and also personal to the individual teacher (Garner & Kaplan, 2019).

A key theory of teacher knowledge development is the notion of reflective practice (Schön, 1983) where teachers engage in 'reflection-on-action' and 'reflection-in-action'. Through engaging in reflection, teachers become researchers of their own practice in their context, generating knowledge and expertise that enables them to respond to different practices and problems in their teaching. Teachers construct personal theories in and from practice. This theory treats teacher knowledge as situational and contextual, yet implies a certain level of knowledge that enables a teacher to notice and make reasoned judgements about practice.

Reflection is also a core component of several other models of teacher learning. Clarke and Hollingsworth's interconnected model of professional growth (2002) includes the processes of reflection and enactment to describe the connections between teacher knowledge and their practice, as well as with their goals and the context in which they are teaching. Orchard and Winch (Orchard & Winch, 2015) proposed a distinct two-stage process of initial teacher education beginning with a focus on practical experience, with theoretical and academic input alongside opportunities for critical reflection included in the second stage. This resonates with the role of reflection in another model of teacher learning, practical theorizing, which argues that teachers need some knowledge to make sense of what they are reflecting on or in.

Practical theorizing is an idea that encapsulates a process of professional learning developed and used at our own institution as well as more widely. This idea arose out of the debates around the relationship between theory and practice, a relationship we will return to later in this chapter. A central tenet of practical theorizing is that 'all suggestions for practice, regardless of whether they derived from research or from practical experience in specific context' are treated as hypotheses to be tested (Burn et al., 2022, p. 17). That is, both knowledge arising through experience and knowledge arising through theory and research should be considered critically. Critical reflection therefore not only plays an essential role in practical theorizing, but it also goes beyond reflection-on- and -in-practice to include suggestions for practice arising from theory and research.

Practical, Theoretical or Professional Teacher Knowledge

Teacher knowledge or teacher knowing is central to many of the debates around the relationship between theory and practice. There is currently general agreement that effective teaching involves both practical skills and theoretical understandings but the relationship between these and the roles each play in teacher learning are still widely debated. What can teachers learn from educational research? Should teachers actively engage with this research or is it the responsibility of researchers and curriculum designers to mediate the research through professional development and/or curricula materials? If, when and how does educational research need to be adapted for the specific contexts in which teachers are working?

Distinctions can also be made within the nature of teacher knowledge around practical knowledge that is grounded in experiences and theoretical or formal knowledge (e.g. Gess-Newsome, 2015; Winch et al., 2015). These distinctions are particularly evident in the different approaches to contingent knowledge, knowledge-in-use or knowing-to which focus on the actions of teachers. For example, teachers can develop their handling of student errors or misconceptions in multiple ways, including through their experiences of students making these errors or holding these misconceptions and how they handled these experiences: reflecting on and adapting to their experience and perception of how 'successful' they were, and developing their knowledge of how to respond to student error (i.e. through critical reflection). From another perspective, teachers might develop this knowledge by working on examples of student errors and misconceptions identified through research and considering alternative approaches to handling these, drawing on research and literature that advocates for particular approaches. And to give a third option, teachers might develop this knowledge by observing 'expert' or the 'best' teachers and learning from them.

Drawing on all of these different knowledges is emphasized in the BERA-RSA (2014) report into the role of research in teacher education which describes teachers as professionals who have the 'capacity to integrate knowledge from different sources, and apply and adopt in practice' (p. 7). The report identifies three sources of this knowledge: subject and pedagogical knowledge, practical experience, and research literacy. A diversity and breadth of knowledges – emphasizing the 'both-and' conception of the knowledges teachers need against a reductionist and simply 'technical' account is a theme across the different contributions to the BERA-RSA report. For example, Winch, Oancea and Orchards (2015) identify three interconnected and complementary aspects of teachers' professional knowledge. Specifically, it is the combination of practical wisdom, technical knowledge and critical reflection that marks teachers out as professionals. Cochran-Smith and Lytle's (1999) early conceptualization of teacher knowledge proposes that teachers must possess and operationalize knowledge on two planes: knowledge-*for*-practice ('know what') referring to the theoretical aspects of teacher knowledge and knowledge-*in*-practice ('know how') referring to the experiential aspects. They then add knowledge-*of*-practice which is a type of local knowledge where teachers intentionally investigate their own classrooms and school within the context of knowledge-for-practice and knowledge-in-practice.

Bernstein's description of vertical and horizontal discourses of knowledge (1999) has also been influential in many discussions about knowledge (including powerful knowledge discussed in Chapter 4 and concerns around social inequality discussed in Chapter 5). For Bernstein, 'horizontal discourse' is local, context specific and dependent, 'common sense' knowledge, embedded in practice. This connects to the ideas of 'know how' teacher knowledge discussed earlier. In contrast, 'vertical discourse' is formal, coherent and specialized knowledge. This type of knowledge is that which is developed through the practices of formal educational research, mediated by peer-review and norms about what counts as rigorous and quality research. This connects to the ideas around 'know why' knowledge discussed earlier.

The role of 'common sense' features in many of these discussions around teacher knowledge. Over time, through practical experience, teachers develop intuitions that enable them to act in the moment. This idea is at the heart of the notion of teaching as a craft. However, the lack of consensus between teachers on 'common sense' thinking, as well as the occurrence of widely held teacher ideas treated as 'common sense' that have been contracted or challenged by research, has led to many arguing for the importance of theory (Orchard & Winch, 2015) or external mentors (McIntyre & Hobson, 2016) in developing these intuitions. The central theme of these arguments is that teacher knowledge is complex, and to be developed well it needs to be informed by a critical engagement with a wide range of different types of knowledge.

The relevance of educational research to teachers' practice is widely supported and critiqued (Winch et al., 2015), and there are tensions between the rapid growth and popularity of the idea of research (particularly through organizations such as ResearchED), and a rejection of many types of research. Ideas about what counts as 'proper' research through which knowledge about teaching is produced continue to echo the discourses around Randomised Controlled Trials being the gold standard of research described by Furlong (2004). He describes the popularity of a 'big science' model and policy for research, contrasts this against a diverse range of other methodological and epistemological options, and defends a 'rich and diverse range of approaches to research, promoting debate about quality within different sub-communities and encouraging open discussion across epistemological and methodological boundaries' (p. 343).

Yet there are also a diverse range of teacher research initiatives endorsing and supporting teachers to research their own practice, their own contexts and issues that are relevant to them. These range from being university-led (e.g. master's level qualifications), university-school partnerships (e.g. Burn et al., 2021; Penuel et al., 2015) or school-or teacher-led activities that engage with research (e.g. the Chartered College of Teaching; Godfrey, 2016; Mcgann et al., n.d.).

The argument about diversity of knowledges is useful across educational research, and particularly in the context of teacher education. The complexity of teacher knowledge means that it needs to be informed by multiple types of knowledge, from the insights offered by big data, statistical analyses of huge data sets, Systematic Reviews and Randomised Controlled Trials, to the rich descriptions of individual cases, ethnographic observations and in-depth insights that are highly sensitive to contextually specific intricacies. Observation of teachers is an aspect or methodology that is engaged with quite differently across different traditions of research and practice. Yet, when researchers, teacher educators and teachers observe teaching they are observing what teachers do, but not what they are thinking and why they are doing what they do.

Teacher Knowledge and Teaching

These frameworks and models of teacher knowledge (or knowing) have been used and criticized for endorsing particular teaching approaches, cultural values and accepted norms around teaching and learning in particular contexts (Tirosh et al., 2011; Winch et al., 2015). Teaching is an inherently moral activity (Kennedy, 2004), with teachers making decisions that are based on the values as well as their knowledge. Teachers' values, beliefs and orientations will influence the decisions they make. This often forms the basis for the arguments made against the idea of teachers learning solely through practice, or through observing practice or through drawing upon common sense ideas around teaching: teachers whose decisions are made solely through critical reflection on their own practice, or the practice of others are likely to perpetuate beliefs and values that may have been refuted by research, or even been shown to be damaging to students' learning. Take for example the idea of the relationships between teachers' expectations of their students and the idea of a self-fulfilling prophecies, alongside practices such as grouping students by attainment or exclusionary discourses around race, ethnicity or disability.

This perspective of teaching as a moral activity provokes further debate around the question of what knowledge teachers need. In Chapters 4 and 5 we address issues around powerful knowledge, equality and diversity. Do teachers need to know about the debates in these issues? Do they need to engage themselves in these issues? Our own research begins with the assumption that they do, but in ways that are consistent with a practical theorizing approach to teacher learning (e.g. Burn et al., 2016, 2022; Puttick & Wynn, 2021).

In this chapter, we have provided a brief overview of some of the key perspectives on teacher knowledge and the debates that these different perspectives influence. The questions we asked at the beginning of this chapter have only been partially answered by these different perspectives, and we have illustrated the contested nature of these answers. But these discussions raise another fundamental question: Are these models and frameworks useful – not only to teacher educators, but to teachers themselves? When teachers talk about their knowledge do they find talking about it in terms of PCK, or reflection-in-action, or knowledge for teaching helpful in making sense of their own practice and/or development?

CHAPTER 5

Power and Knowledge

Longstanding analyses of the relations between power and knowledge (Bruner, 1970; Delpit, 2011) have recently been brought together in the discourses surrounding *powerful knowledge* (Young & Lambert, 2014). Internationally, powerful knowledge has gained traction, often in combination with notions of cultural capital and cultural literacy, to address the questions: What is the aim of schooling? What knowledge is most worth teaching? Based on distinctions between different types of knowledge, including knowledge of the powerful/powerful knowledge and everyday/disciplinary, powerful knowledge sets out to establish what knowledge is most valuable for students to learn, particularly in relation to claims about social justice. This chapter develops a novel understanding of powerful knowledge as a cluster concept, and then analyses the functions of powerful knowledge in policy discourses across a range of international cases. It then moves to examine critiques of powerful knowledge, including conceptual and definitional issues (White, 2019), the 'shadow and shine' of knowledge (Rudolph et al., 2018) and distinctions between everyday and powerful knowledges (Catling & Martin, 2011). Through this discussion we explore the potential of *disciplinary literacy* to expand discourse, policy, practice and research. We also consider the alternative concept of 'worthwhile' knowledge (Bruner, 1970).

Powerful Knowledge and Crises

In making the case for powerful knowledge, Young has described multiple crises to which powerful knowledge is framed as the solution. One crisis concerns social justice: the injustices of schooling systems that only give some children (wealthier ones) access to more valuable forms of knowledge. Another crisis is in curriculum and curriculum theory, in which he argues that attention to knowledge has been marginalized. Young (2013b) argues that some knowledge is powerful because it provides the best understanding of the natural and social worlds that we have and helps us go beyond our individual experiences; even the creative and performing arts, and literature and drama, have these emergent and universalizing properties, albeit not based on generalizations. Access to powerful knowledge in its diverse forms is an entitlement for all pupils and students. That is why the extent to which a curriculum is underpinned by 'powerful knowledge' is both an epistemological and a social justice issue (p. 196).

The crisis in curriculum is presented by Young (2013a) through a dramatic framing, sketching a number of major claims about trends in education, including

(1)   the distrust in specialization as the primary source of new knowledge in any field;

(2)   the massive expansion of schooling has led, in a contradictory way, to a loss of confidence in its potentially emancipatory role;

(3)   the increasingly widespread acceptance among educational researchers of the idea that knowledge itself has no intrinsic significance or validity. (p.106)

Young then reports conversations with his colleagues who work in teacher education:

University colleagues of mine who visit student teachers in schools report something akin to a 'fear of knowledge' in the schools they visit – knowledge is either not mentioned or seen as something intimidating and dominating. (p. 107)

This is a fascinating – if infuriating! – claim to make: Who in these schools is accused of these things? How do Young's colleagues know? Did Young's colleagues frame their comments in these exact terms, or has a liberal interpretation been applied? Either way, this cannot be a functional basis on which to build the generalizations that Young goes on to make about 'knowledge itself' and the place of knowledge in school curricula. It is also ironic that attempts to argue for powerful knowledge assuming a central role are made on the basis of such obviously non-powerful forms of knowledge.

Paradoxically, Young's use of these anecdotal conversations might function to support his criticism of everyday knowledge, the concepts of which are 'tied to particular contexts, and ... are inevitably limited to those contexts and those experiences' (p. 110). This one example also opens up questions that permeate discussions about knowledge: How do we come to know? Through what kinds of methods can we build knowledge? What types of knowledge do we trust? Why? Who decides? What do these words mean in this context? What other words might someone else have used, and what are the implications of these particular choices? We are also brought immediately into issues of power, and in Young's terms, we might say that these claims about schools do not count as powerful knowledge because they are not produced through rigorous disciplinary methods, but instead are examples of knowledge of the powerful. Yet the distinction between powerful knowledge and knowledge of the powerful falters; the claims are published in highly regarded, peer-reviewed journals and are presented in ways that align with other powerful knowledge criteria (such as claiming to be about the real-world and being produced in specialist disciplinary communities). The point, explored further later, is that those producing disciplinary knowledges are powerful; knowledge of the powerful and powerful knowledge are deeply intertwined and it is not clear that these categories effectively distinguish between different types of knowledge. But before exploring this further, what is powerful knowledge, and how is it defined?

Defining Powerful Knowledge

The concept of powerful knowledge has been defined in two main ways: negatively, in opposition to that which it is not (in particular, it is *not* everyday knowledge); and through lists of characteristics (e.g. it is testable, about the real world, and normally produced in specialist disciplinary communities). Young does not define powerful knowledge through a positive proposition expressing the core of its meaning. Instead, the use of lists of characteristics to define powerful knowledge means that we might think of it as a cluster concept. An example of a cluster concept is developed by Wittgenstein (1958) through his discussion of games. He argues that there is nothing common to all games, for example: some are played on boards, but not all; some involve winning and losing, but not all; some involve skill – which means different things in different games – and others luck. Instead, we know what games are – and we have an idea about what someone means when they mention 'games' – through a cluster of similarities and relationships. Using this kind of definition means that we do not (or cannot) know the defining essence of the concept, but instead we can come to know and identify the concept through a series of characteristics, relations and functions, none of which are necessary or individually sufficient. The lists of criteria associated with powerful knowledge has included statements about it being:

- Conceptual as well as based on evidence and experience;

- Systematically revisable;

- Emergent;

- Material and social;
- About the real world;
- Reliable and in a broad sense 'testable' explanations or ways of thinking;
- Always open to challenge;
- Organised into domains with boundaries that are not arbitrary and these domains are associated with specialist communities such as subject and professional associations;
- Normally (but not always) discipline-based.

(Young & Lambert, 2014; Young & Muller, 2013)

The nature of powerful knowledge as a cluster concept is related to issues around the definition of the term that have been raised by others, particularly White (2018, 2019). The critique focuses on the ways in which powerful knowledge has been enthusiastically taken up in policy debates but as a soundbite with limited clarity or substance. Our description of powerful knowledge as a cluster concept is not an evaluative account – using a cluster concept is not necessarily a bad thing – but it does point to the ambiguity and therefore limitations of powerful knowledge as a principle around which schools and curricula might be designed. Using the examples of 'games' as a cluster concept, *shall we play a game?* is one kind of question, but it does not get you much closer to deciding what to do. What type of game? Which game shall we play? What counts as 'a game', and what kinds of activities are excluded as not-games?

Having previously rejected 'esoteric' definitions, Muller and Young's (2019) more recent arguments around powerful knowledge rely on a Latin distinction, drawn from Spinoza, between *potentia* (power to) and *potestas* (power over). The latter – *potestas* – is 'the traditional notion of power as domination of one agent over another . . . always deformative, it withdraws, excludes or deprives', whereas *potentia* is 'productive or creative, it extends horizons, it imagines new futures' (p. 201). They argue that powerful knowledge is this latter type of knowledge: 'power in the sense of its augmentative, enhancing and empowering capacity' (p. 209). The arguments laid out by White (2019) in *The End of Powerful Knowledge* highlights Muller and Young's new way of defining powerful knowledge:

> the descriptive meaning they have attached to the word has totally altered. . . . This reinforces the suspicion that, consciously or unconsciously, they have been attracted from the start by the non-descriptive, emotive connotation of the term [powerful knowledge] as something unquestionably worth having. (p. 437)

Quite bluntly, White argues for abandoning the phrase 'powerful knowledge' and replacing it with 'terminology appropriate to impartial scholarly investigation rather than language more at home in the world of product promotion' (p. 437). An aspect of 'product promotion' characterizing powerful knowledge is the silence around problematic – *potestas* – aspects of academic disciplines. An important critique of powerful knowledge is related to its normative position: powerful knowledge, and the disciplines through which this knowledge is produced, are presented uncritically as good. But as many have now suggested, the traditions through which disciplines have emerged and continued to build are far more complex than this. Before exploring conceptual issues around the ways in which powerful knowledge defines knowledge as something separate from belief, we explore the 'shadow and shine' of knowledge further.

Shadow and Shine of Knowledge

Powerful knowledge relies on a highly positive account of academic disciplines. They are praised for being the most reliable and authoritative producers of knowledge: 'they represent the best that has been thought in that realm of ideas' (Muller & Young, 2019). The knowledge produced by disciplines is contrasted against everyday knowledge, and giving students access to this powerful knowledge is argued to be the defining aim of schooling. However, this positive framing ignores important questions about the nature of disciplinary knowledge and education, and some of the deeply problematic ways in which disciplines have been tied up with racist colonial pasts and presents. In Gerrard et al.'s (2022) terms,

> education is central to the production and reproduction of racial inequalities globally. Systems of formal education cannot be separated from colonial and national projects that have sought to categorise, divide, oppress, enslave, and assimilate people on the basis of race. (p. 425)

These knowledges are certainly powerful, but this is not a kind of power that is obviously or even mostly good. As Mignolo (2011) puts it, disciplines produce both 'shadow and shine', and there are tensions between education's 'complicity in maintaining unjust hierarchies against its potential for emancipatory transformation' (Puttick et al., 2022, p. 1). Conceptions of powerful knowledge have focused on the shine while ignoring the shadow. In Rudolph et al.'s (2018, p. 22) terms, 'powerful knowledge seems to focus on the progressive impulse of modernity (its "shine") while overlooking the ruination of colonial racism (its "shadow")'. There are multiple forms of shadow which vary between disciplines and in different ways through the development of their practices, knowledges and traditions. Obvious examples include the ways in which disciplines such as geography have been bound up with and used to support imperial projects of domination: powerful knowledge, for example, of mapping and classifications, through which to dominate and exploit others.

To give one geographical example, Halford Mackinder – who founded the school of Geography at the University of

Oxford (SoGE, 2019) – has been shown to have used geography to develop highly racist ideas in support of British imperialism, to have developed accounts of environmental determinism that were used and enthusiastically taken up by Nazi Germany, and to have had African porters murdered (Kearns, 2009, 2020). Messy entanglements between disciplines, knowledge and empire. Yet Mackinder continues to hold an authoritative role in many aspects of the subject, including recently being uncritically held up in Ofsted's (Office for Standards in Education, Children's Services and Skills) research report on geography (Ofsted, 2021). These are non-trivial examples of shadow, of disciplines and disciplinary knowledge production steeped in *potestas* with which current practice is only just beginning to grapple. Theoretical engagements, such as through postcolonialism, produce generative ways to think about and navigate the production of knowledge, which is vital, 'given that we work in a planetary context so striated by colonialism' (Jazeel, 2019, p. 197). Such grappling with the shadow side of disciplines and knowledge is part of what we explore later through the notion of *disciplinary literacy* and then further in Chapter 6.

Social Justice

The problematic shadow aspects of disciplines are one part of the arguments that have been made around social justice, mainly epistemic justice. While powerful knowledge discourse has largely ignored those aspects of epistemic justice in relation to academic disciplines and knowledge production, it has foregrounded aims of social justice. This foregrounding is summarized by Francis et al. (2017) as raising 'concerns about marginalized groups of students missing out on powerful forms of knowledge' (p. 419), where the power comes from knowledge's exchange value and provision of other forms of capital in the workplace. In Young's (2013b) terms, 'access to powerful knowledge in its diverse forms is an entitlement for all pupils and students. That is why the extent to which a curriculum is underpinned by "powerful knowledge" is both an epistemological and a social justice issue' (p. 196). The arguments for making powerful knowledge available to all students are in part driven by dichotomies that have underpinned debates around knowledge in education, summarized by Francis et al. (2017, p. 417) as:

Vocational	vs.	Academic
Skills	vs.	Knowledge
Progressive	vs.	Traditional
Soft	vs.	Hard
Dumbed down	vs.	Rigour
Mass	vs.	Elite
Arts & humanities	vs.	Sciences
Body	vs.	Mind
Enquiry	vs.	Facts
Extrinsic	vs.	Intrinsic

They describe one tension between 'locally relevant/ engaging curricula vs. national entitlement to "high status knowledge"' (p. 421), arguing that while relevant, they are often undervalued and underrecognized in formal education systems, despite the fact that local knowledges and experiences have been shown to drive engagement and social justice. Consequently 'if these "local knowledges" differ from high status and / or difficult knowledge, the provision of "engaging" curricula to disadvantaged/marginalized children may further entrench their disadvantage by precluding access to high status education and career paths' (p. 421). Here, power is associated with the power of accreditation: this is not an argument about the intrinsic value of one type of knowledge over another, but instead focuses on what the recognition of one type of knowledge can buy. Because socio-economic background continues to be the strongest predictor of academic success

(Fiel, 2020), this social justice argument seems to be an urgent task.

This same argument that is behind the knowledge is power program (KIPP) in Charter Schools in the United States, founded in the 1990s by two Teach for America graduates, frustrated at the difficulties of closing the attainment gap for students, in terms of both socio-economic and racial disparities in attainment. The programme works on the principle of massively increasing instructional time in high school, with a focus on standardized attainment scores. One critic of KIPP has argued that KIPP 'merely preserves the status quo by asking students to overcome overwhelming disparities through – hard work and – motivation, instead of addressing the structural sources of poverty and poor academic achievement – i.e., the unequal distribution of resources in schools and society. By subscribing to a dictum of no excuses, KIPP essentially puts the onus on the victims of poverty and institutional racism' (Lack, 2009, p. 127).

Similarly, an important part of Francis et al.'s (2017) argument focuses on the importance of conceptual clarity and the recognition that addressing injustice is not straightforward. The simple binaries between powerful/everyday and knowledge of the powerful/powerful knowledge limits both: the potential for richer, more critical understandings of disciplines to inform school subjects, and the potential for children's experiences, understandings and beliefs to meaningfully connect with and inform their education. Therefore, we want to challenge the ways in which some of these debates and tensions have been portrayed through powerful knowledge discourses. For example, in the way that Young and Lambert (2014) argue that differentiating knowledge according to these kinds of dichotomies is an important task for educators:

> we start with [the] view that as educators, we must differentiate types of knowledge: in particular between the knowledge that pupils bring to school and the knowledge

that the curriculum gives them access to. This view does not involve any esoteric distinctions. (p. 14)

We want to challenge the nature of this distinction, and the nature of the relationships and hierarchies between these different types of knowledge. Instead, we want to suggest a more expansive and ambitious ideal in which all young people are given access to disciplinary literacies in ways that meaningfully engage with, relate to, are informed – and even challenged and refined – by the knowledges they already bring to school. Knowledges believed and justified to varying degrees.

Knowledge, Belief and Experience

Throughout the history of philosophy, knowledge has been defined closely in relation to belief. An influential definition presents knowledge through three conditions: as justified true belief (Dutant, 2015). Responses to this *justified true belief* definition have focused mainly on the condition of justification. Knowledge is overwhelmingly held to be something about or in relation to truth, however thorny defining truth has been across the social sciences and humanities. Similarly, to know something is widely understood to mean having some kind of commitment; believing, or being sure (to various degrees) about something. The justification condition has attracted most attention, including through 'Gettier problems' (Gettier, 1963), which raise questions about the role epistemic luck plays; for example, if my belief is true, but not properly justified because it is based on false beliefs, does this still count as knowledge? A notion of belief is also important to the tradition of virtue epistemology that we began this book with, in which knowledge has been defined as 'belief arising out of acts of intellectual virtue' (Zagzebski, 1999, p. 109). *Belief* is explicitly included in these definitions of knowledge. Whereas, Young and Lambert's (2014, p. 17) insistence that knowledge, experience and belief are distinct raises some issues, including through their arguments for knowledge as something universal, which means that 'unlike common sense, [knowledge] is never something "given" and *never* tied to specific contexts' (p. 17). The distinction between everyday experience and knowledge is too simple, but what do they mean by experience? 'Experience is just experience – what we are' (p.18). In opposition to this,

> Unlike gaining a new experience, acquiring . . . 'powerful knowledge' always requires much dedicated effort and hard work . . . Knowledge, like anything worthwhile, is not only shared but has to be struggled for – wrought from the world by work no less dedicated than the work it took to create it. (p. 18)

The deeply classed and racialized experiences of schooling and academic attainment suggest that blanket statements about how much effort and hard work is required to gain knowledge are not true. The different levels of effort and hard work required by different people is an important and underexplored dimension of the relationships between everyday and powerful knowledge. It is also not always (or even normally) the case that coming to know these knowledges produced by others requires dedication equal to the work it took to create it. Again, the specificity of individuals' experiences and prior knowledge makes all of the difference. For us to come to know the height of Everest would take far less dedication than the measuring and fieldwork that it took to create that knowledge. The measurement of that particular height is also a whole other story tied up with imperial power, epistemic and social injustices and power inequalities that illustrate well some of the shadow side of disciplinary knowledges (Fleetwood, 2022). Who actually created this knowledge, and who is credited as having created it? The co-production of knowledge is often hidden (Driver, 2013), and Fleetwood's analysis of Himalayan mapping offers one example of the contested nature of knowledge construction and representation that opens up not only the 'dedicated' work taken to construct the knowledge, but also the messy politics and power imbalances. There are important senses in which this knowledge, not only but including the mountain's height, are most definitely tied to specific contexts. The knowledge that Fleetwood has produced of the processes and politics is tied to specific contexts in ways that contribute to the richness, depth and specificity of the knowledge. It is not a view from nowhere. The idea of 'struggling' to construct knowledge needs to be pushed further and seen as not necessarily or exclusively a good thing. It would also be naïve to assume that these shadow sides of knowledge construction are limited to colonial expeditions in the Himalaya. Today's laboratories, learned societies, academic conferences and publishing are similarly human and shot through with inequalities and injustices, even if the manifestations of shadow take different forms.

Powerful Knowledge and Policymaking in England

The review of the National Curriculum in England was led in 2011 by an expert panel who made it clear that 'powerful knowledge' was their driving principle: they worked with 'a particular focus on clear and well evidenced "maps" of the key elements of subjects – giving all pupils access to "powerful knowledge"' (Department for Education, 2011, p. 11). At a basic level, some underlying assumptions behind powerful knowledge might be seen in the shape curriculum reform has taken. For example, this national curriculum is structured around subjects (rather than themes or other organizing principles), reflecting the value placed on subjects and disciplinary expertise.

Furthermore, Ofsted's interventions in policy discourse and the practice of schools and settings exert strong levels of control (Cushing & Snell, 2022), acting as a key knowledge broker, establishing some forms and sources of knowledge as valuable and authoritative and others as worthless. Their shaping of policy discourse happens through many channels, including the publication of inspection reports; summaries of management information; speeches; blog posts; and social media (among others). The way curriculum is inspected carries through this prioritization of subject-specific knowledge and skills.

At the heart of the ongoing struggles around curriculum reform in England is a fundamental contradiction between rhetoric about powerful knowledge which places the highest value on knowledge produced through academic disciplines and an aggressive marketization of ITE (Initial Teacher Education) which has sought to undermine and reduce university involvement (Mincu & Davies, 2019). Teaching is powerful, and various culture wars around what is taught (with prominent recent examples including critical race theory and the supposed 'banning' of particular books) illustrate the strength with which beliefs about the importance of teaching – and ITE – are held.

Disciplinary knowledge is not a silver bullet. McPhail and Rata (2016) claim that 'although disciplinary knowledge is created by people, it is objective, not subjective, because it uses universalised concepts created in the disciplinary communities, and this provisional knowledge is subject to rules and procedures which continually test the truth claims' (p. 55). This does not describe any arts, humanities, social or natural sciences. No truth claims are continually tested in any disciplinary community. The relationship between objectivity and subjectivity is far more complex and far trickier to define (let alone establish consensus around) than this simplistic dichotomy reveals.

There are also questions about time: Is disciplinary knowledge always objective? Or when we look back and see that maybe it was just wrong, does it then stop being objective and instead become a situated, subjective perspective? Some of these challenges are illustrated in the geographical example of Halford Mackinder discussed earlier. A notion of disciplinary literacy, developed further later after a brief discussion of powerful knowledge and the curriculum, may help to develop a more nuanced, critical and reflexive approach towards engaging with disciplinary knowledges. The aspiration of disciplinary literacy articulated later has implications for across education systems including a challenge for those involved with accountability regimes, inspecting and governing education.

Powerful Knowledge and the Curriculum: South Africa, Rwanda and New Zealand

Young's distinction between powerful knowledge and everyday knowledge has been used to drive policymaking and to structure the analysis of curricula in a range of international contexts. For example, the strongly defended dichotomies that powerful knowledge relies on characterizes some of the debate around New Zealand's curricular reforms, including contrasts between Powerful Knowledge and 21st Century Learning (McPhail & Rata, 2016). In their analysis of New Zealand's curriculum policy – particularly the Ministry of Education's promotion of 'identity affirming culturally responsive pedagogical initiatives' (p. 392) and Māori students' educational ('under') achievement – Lynch and Rata (2018) apply a binary distinction between powerful and everyday knowledge. Drawing on Bernstein, they use the terms 'vertical' (academic) and 'horizontal' (everyday) knowledges, with the former being defined as 'coherent, explicit and systematically principled' and the latter 'context dependent sociocultural knowledge' (p. 392). They are highly critical of the way in which 'many educational researchers . . . believe that the solution for raising the educational achievement of indigenous and other minority groups, is through a curriculum which mostly incorporates a sociocultural horizontal knowledge' (p. 392). Their claim about what 'many educational researchers' believe has the same obvious problems we discussed earlier in relation to Young's claims about what his colleagues anecdotally

reported from schools. This is not a minor issue because
the whole framing of powerful knowledge as a curriculum
solution that will save Māori young people is built on populist
dichotomies that strongly echo attacks against university-based
teacher educators as 'the blob' elsewhere (Craske, 2021). The
distinction between vertical and horizontal knowledges is also
problematic. For example, to what extent does the description
of academic knowledge accurately represent real-world
academic disciplines. Is disciplinary knowledge 'coherent'?
Maybe within a single journal article, but across even a single
issue of a journal there are often sharp disagreements and
'coherent' would not be an appropriate descriptor; 'contested'
might be more accurate. And at the other end, is everyday
knowledge not coherent? There are good arguments to
suggest that *coherence* of beliefs might be more common in
everyday knowledges than within heterogeneous disciplines.
For example, see Chipeniuk's (1998) discussion of theories
of Spring to illustrate some of the complexity across 'lay',
'scientific' and other types of knowledges and explanations.

New Zealand's curricular reforms have brought these
debates around knowledge into sharp relief. Te Hurihanganui
(Ministry of Education, 2021) is explicitly framed as a
decolonial, co-designed approach that recognizes the existence
of 'rich and legitimate knowledge' within a Māori world view,
and holds that this knowledge must be given space in the
curriculum. The aim is to:

> Support communities to work together to address racism
> and inequity so that they can accelerate the achievement
> and wellbeing of ākonga Māori and their whānau. What
> works in communities will then be built back into the
> education system so that we see transformative shift for all
> ākonga Māori and their whānau throughout the education
> system. (Ministry of Education, 2021)

Placing Māori knowledges – everyday, 'horizontal' –
knowledges on an equal footing in the curriculum conflicts

with the ideals articulated through powerful knowledge approaches, which Rata's response to curricular reform in New Zealand illustrates. She argues that

> A revolution is coming. The Government's transformational policies for education make this clear. It will only be stopped by a re-commitment to academic knowledge for all New Zealand children, rich and poor alike, within a universal and secular education system. Colonisation is not the problem and decolonisation is not the solution. (Rata, 2022)

Disciplinary Literacy

We want to suggest that *disciplinary literacy* is a good alternative to the concept and rhetoric of powerful knowledge. By creating space for more critical, nuanced understandings of academic knowledges and their histories, disciplinary literacy is able to hold both that colonization is a major problem, decolonization is an important part of the solution, and that disciplinary knowledges in all of their shadow and shine continue to offer vibrant and empowering resources and conversations to which all young people ought to be given access. Drawing on Rudolph et al.'s (2018) use of the 'shadow and shine' of knowledge to critically examine the relations between power and knowledge, and the problematic features of powerful knowledge policy discourses identified through this chapter, we now expand on the discussion about subjects and disciplines in Chapter 4 to suggest that an idea of disciplinary literacy offers greater potential to expand discourse, policy and practice in ways that may currently be restricted by ideas about powerful knowledge.

Our point in highlighting problematic, shadow aspects of disciplines and knowledge is not a call for 'ignoring' knowledge, or for a kind of relativism as Rata and others (e.g. Young & Lambert, 2014) suggest, but is instead about more honestly facing and uncovering these uncomfortable histories and presents. In *Provincializing Europe*, Chakrabarty (2000) writes that his argument is not about 'rejecting or discarding' European knowledges and ways of thinking – it is a kind of 'postcolonial revenge', because

> European thought is at once both indispensable and inadequate in helping us to think through the experiences of political modernity in non-Western nations, and provincializing Europe becomes the task of exploring how this thought – which is now everybody's heritage and which affect us all – may be renewed from and for the margins. (p. 17)

Developing disciplinary literacy is hard and places demands involving wrestling with the tensions between disciplines as both indispensable and inadequate. The notion of disciplinary literacy reframes the work of teacher education more explicitly at the interface between academic disciplines and school subjects. Teachers have an important role to play in facilitating and mediating this relationship and in its renewal. One reason this challenge is so hard is because of the dynamic nature of academic disciplines: they change, sometimes radically and sometimes imperceptibly. They are also heterogeneous, which means it is hard to capture the essence of a discipline in any straightforward sense across time and space. Some of the changes within disciplines come about as a reaction to previous work, and at other times through responses to events, movements and arguments developed and happing outside the discipline. These shifts are sometimes called 'turns', and so we hear about spatial, social, digital, cultural turns and more. Fragments of past traditions and schools of thought continue, while other aspects are left behind.

One aspect of developing 'disciplinary literacy', and of making this a priority in schools, is introducing students to a sense of the nature of a discipline. To do this, we make simplifications and use generalizations, naming broad sweeps of time through one label representing a dominant school of thought, quantitative revolution, non-representational theory, affective turn and so on. These kinds of labels help us to domesticate the arguments, contradictions and variety within disciplines as the subject shifts and evolves. The labels and stories that we tell about disciplines also buy into a belief in progress; it seems obvious that we know more now than we did before. Between us writing these words and this book being published, millions of other books will have been published, countless blog posts written, tweets sent and experiments conducted. We will know more then than we do now. However, is it that simple? Does 'more' in this case mean that we will actually know more? And who does the 'we' refer to? Becoming literate about a discipline includes addressing questions about difference and change as much as progress and development. The scale and complexity of the task for teacher education at the interface between academic disciplines and school subjects should not be underestimated!

Worthwhile Knowledge

In this chapter we have considered the relationship between power and knowledge. In particular the cluster construct of powerful knowledge, its influences and its critique, arguing for disciplinary literacy as an alternative construct. We now end this chapter by turning to work of Jerome Bruner who challenges us to think about what makes knowledge worthwhile in and of itself, not as a waypoint en route to an academic qualification, not as a representation of the currency it can buy or the points it can accrue:

> We might ask, as a criterion for any subject taught in primary school, whether, when fully developed, it is worth an adult's knowing, and whether having known it as a child makes a person a better adult . . . it should follow that a curriculum ought to be built around the great issues, principles and values that a society deems worthy of the continual concerns of its members. (1960, p. 52)

CHAPTER 6

Knowledge for All

Throughout this book we have highlighted questions about who gets to define what knowledge is accepted as valuable. Chapter 1 opened questions about value in relation to how knowledge is defined and economic narratives reducing knowledge's worth to monetary exchange value. Chapter 2 then situated debates about knowledge in relation to students' experiences of education, highlighting some of the differences between subjects, disciplines and traditions of knowledge. The increasingly significant role that large tech companies play in making certain types of information visible through algorithmically mediated, personalized search results, and the relationships between these technologies and knowledge in teacher education, was explored in Chapter 3. Chapter 4 then foregrounded teachers' roles in the selection and transformation of the knowledge they make accessible to students, drawing particular attention to the significant dimension of teachers' subject-specific expertise. Arguments about the 'shadow and shine' of knowledge in Chapter 5 then framed these questions about who gets to decide what knowledge is accepted and valued in a particular way that emphasizes the tensions between knowledge as emancipatory – a liberating, progressive force for good in the world – and knowledge as oppressive – enforcing social reproduction and inequality that is deeply racialized, classed and gendered. In this chapter we develop a notion of *knowledge for all* in teacher education.

Who are the 'all'? And what different ideas do we bring to our engagements with knowledge? The individual background each person brings to what they see has a huge impact on what they perceive; in Oxford where the authors work there are community allotments close to the railway station – council-owned plots of land which local people can rent for a nominal amount to grow fruit and vegetables. They frequently have a patchwork of sheds, greenhouses and makeshift tool-sheds on them so that people can leave equipment there, or have a quiet sit with a cup of tea in peace. Visitors from overseas, arriving by train in Oxford, often perceive these allotments as slums. Small, makeshift buildings, not very watertight, with evidence of subsistence farming on a small-scale. What does your background enable or prevent you from seeing in the material you meet?

Educational Canons

'Canons' are accepted bodies of (essential educational?) knowledge in different fields. The term originates from biblical studies, where it denotes the set of books which constitute the Bible. The term is then used by analogy for the set of literature texts that are worth studying, and from there into other subjects. Ironically, for a term which is often considered to mean 'the one, official set of texts', in biblical studies the canon can vary dramatically between different Jewish and Christian denominations.

Some argue that canons derive from objective definitions of quality, like the critic Harold Bloom, who in his *The Western Canon* insists on aesthetic value being the only criterion for the canon, and criticizes the 'academic rabble that seeks to connect the study of literature with the quest for social change' (1990, pp. 27–8) (a point to which we will later return). However, our stance is that canons are social formations: in other words they derive from people, not objective standards of value. We concur with John Guillory that canons comprise 'institutional forms of syllabus and curriculum' (Guillory, 1993, p. vii), reproduced and created by educational norms. Macaluso and Macaluso (2018) relate the influence of Harvard University on the emergent school literary curriculum in the United States:

> The 1873-1874 Harvard admissions requirement stated, for the first time, that applicants would write a short composition on a literary text. Because specific titles – ranging from Shakespeare to Sir Walter Scott – were mentioned in the requirement and in subsequent requirements, secondary school teachers felt they had no choice but to teach those specific titles in their classrooms. (Macaluso & Macaluso, 2018, p. xi)

They then note that publishers saw an opportunity and produced annotated versions of many of these texts, beginning the influence of study editions and educational publishers' desire for profit on the educational 'canon'. The canon is somewhat different today, having been updated in part, and different from country to country, but is still largely a socially constructed version of what is valuable to know.

This social and historical construction of canons has serious implications for who and what gets studied and how. Raewyn Connell describes the ways in which the history of sociology (and the world) shaped the discipline to focus on theory which came out of specific Western universities, framing those of the Global South as subjects of research, not its proponents (Connell, 2007). Sociological theories (which include many educational theories) therefore often make claims to be universal but are based on only one half of the world. As an example, she gives the concept of time in social theory: it offers 'the world-time of an intelligible historic succession (pre-modern to modern, pre-capitalist to capitalist, etc.). This is time as experienced in the metropole. In colonised and settler societies, time involves fundamental discontinuity and unintelligible succession' (Connell, 2007, p. 45), because the violence of conquest has broken off gradual societal evolution, and introduced massive dis-conjunctions. Here we see not only how Westernized schooling may clash with Indigenous experiences but also how contingent knowledge can be, depending on the place from which you view it.

Educational research, and research in teacher education, also has established canons; highly cited works that dominate the field and are widely accepted as being a proper part of what counts as knowledge. To give one example, Stephen Ball wrote a BERA (British Educational Research Association) blog (Ball, 2020) in which he listed the ten books that have most influenced him: the ten most important texts that have informed his work and career. As an example of the social formation of canons, Stephen Ball is a good example for a number of reasons: he held a highly prestigious position as the Karl Mannheim professor of sociology of education at UCL/ IoE (University College London/Institute of Education); and his own work has been very widely read and cited (one of his papers – *The Teacher's Soul and the Terrors of Performativity* – has been cited in other work over 6,000 times, and over 20 of his papers or books have each been cited over 1,000 times). A lot of people have read, his work, and a lot of people have used and credited his work. We are among these people, and also go on to add further citations by engaging with some of this work later! None of what we will go on to critically say about the blog and this example of canon-formation should be taken to imply that we do not think his work is exceptional or important. In his BERA blog, which is his account of the ten books that have most influenced him, there are some revealing omissions. Every single one of the ten books that he lists have something in common: they were all written by white men. Why does this matter? In Ball's (2020) words, 'these books are keepers. I will never part with them: they are part of me, of what I think, what I do, how I think, how I do what I do'. What we read, and whose perspectives get to play a part in what we think, how we think, what we do and how we do what we do have many far-reaching implications. These implications include, in the Foucauldian discourse analysis sense that Ball has used elsewhere, setting the terms of the debate: establishing what kinds of things are seen as appropriate to speak about, and the concepts and frameworks through which these discussions might happen.

As Ball has so compellingly argued, governance of educational systems happens in large part through controlling the discourse. This point is at the heart of his analysis of policy networks of globally interconnected actors and institutions producing shared 'sensibilities and worldviews . . . [a] high degree of epistemic homophily' (Ball, 2016, p. 553). That is, shared ideas about what counts as knowledge and how the world works. In the context of policy networks around educational reform in India (highly relevant to the context of teacher education) he argues that these shared ideas are mobilized around 'critiques, and concerns about the efficacy of the state and the ineffectiveness of public education and over and against this an adherence to "casual stories" and "silver bullets" that offer "solutions" to these failures'. Such 'casual stories' and 'silver bullets' include private-public partnerships, entrepreneurship and leadership, and 'measurement and outcomes driven reform'. Ball calls this bundle of ideas neoliberal rationality that 'deploys the techniques of investment, business innovation, and performance management as methods for the re-culturation and re-form of public education' (p. 553). In teacher education we might trace exactly these same logics of neoliberal rationality, particularly through attempted reforms in England and the workings of overlapping networks that have discursively constructed reductionist ideas about what counts as teacher knowledge, what kinds of knowledge should be taught in schools and who gets access to this knowledge. The overwhelmingly technicist assumptions about knowledge attempt to side-line sticky questions about complexity and uncertainty to prioritize standardization and certainty. Similarly, derision of university-based teacher education involves repeating tropes about the ineffectiveness of public education and the need for market-based solutions. What counts as accepted curricular knowledge in teacher education, and who gets to decide this, is highly political and is one part of global policy networks driven by and constructing a neoliberal rationality. Questioning and expanding the canon of what counts as accepted curricular knowledge is (and will always be) an urgent task which has taken on a particular shape amid the current teacher education reforms.

Despite the rhetoric around canonicity, canons can and do shift over time. In the case of literature, the 'canon opening' movement of the late 1970s (see for example Fiedler, 1981) broadly proposed that canon opening 'combats Western epistemic violence; the open canon lets those who have been silenced speak' (McGowan, 2014, p. xii). To 'open' the canon is to deliberately and intentionally incorporate texts from under-represented groups into curricula and syllabuses to ensure their canonization through institutional reproduction. In the 1970s that meant introducing texts by women; now the focus is more broadly on race, gender identity and sexuality. Specific projects include the 1619 project in the United States which reframed American history with a focus on slavery and the contributions of Black Americans, published as long form journalism but with a clear agenda for education. In South Africa and the UK the Rhodes Must Fall (see for example Chantiluke et al., 2018) movements focused on the decolonization of university curricula, as did the Why Is My Curriculum White? campaign at University College, London. In schools the diversification of English literature is promoted by campaigns such as Lit in Colour in the UK (Elliott et al., 2021) or the push for Australian national literature to be taught (Mclean Davies et al., 2022). There can also be pushback against such canon opening, as demonstrated by contemporary campaigns for book banning particularly in relation to LGBTQIA+ content in the United States, a movement which Graff (2022) decries as 'the New Illiteracy' (p. 287).

Educational canons are particularly vulnerable to washback from assessment specifications. Since reform in 2015, the privileging of socio-historic context in examination specifications for English literature in England has meant increased prioritizing of biographical and historical facts in studying English (as noted by Barbara Bleiman of the English and Media Centre), which fits with the 'knowledge turn'. Changes in the topics set for study can also have an impressive impact on what is taught: Edexcel in England has been particularly influential in pushing recognition of diverse perspectives in both English and history. State requirements to study national native literature in Australia, however, have mostly meant the replacement of dead white British authors with white Australians writing in the same tradition, which is not an effective diversification.

A critical movement in the 1970s and 1980s brought an urgent challenge to school geography by highlighting its un(der)examined biases. This critical movement is described in Norcup's (2015) doctoral research on *Awkward Geographies* which foregrounds the vital contribution made by Dawn Gill and colleagues including through the Association for Curriculum Development (ACDG) and journal *Contemporary Issues in Geography and Education*. As part of this movement, Hicks' list of recommendations (reproduced in Walford, 2001, p. 187) argues the geography 'canon' needs shifting:

1   We urgently consider how to bring the 'relevance revolution' into school geography.

2   Educational publishers need to develop checklists and guidelines on ethnocentric bias in geography textbooks a) to use themselves and b) to be used by authors.

3   Educational publishers need to commission new textbooks to rectify the deficient images already noted in this survey.

4   Teachers and study groups need to make known praise or blame for textbooks and make their comments and criteria known to publishers and colleagues.

Ongoing conversations, such as through the *Decolonising Geography* collective (https://decolonisegeography.com)

highlight the similarities between the current situation in school geography and the critical anti-racist and decolonial arguments being made fifty years ago. As Puttick and Murrey (2020) have argued, 'Geography education in England has a problem with race' (p. 126) and in part this argument is about the disconnections between geography as an academic discipline and as a school subject, and the opportunities to expand the canon of school geography by engaging with cutting-edge arguments in the discipline (Esson & Last, 2020). This argument is also about the history of school geography as a subject tied up with colonialism and imperial expeditions to violently conquer and rule others. Addressing (decolonizing) the colonial assumptions that continue to shape the canon of subjects such as geography is an essential task for constructing, recontextualizing and teaching knowledge for all.

What can we learn from these shifts for research and practice in teacher education? In what ways might these past curricular shifts illuminate contemporary opportunities and challenges for constructing curriculum that are diverse, inclusive and accessible for all? One is that deliberate action works, and that what is controversial (such as the incorporation of more female authors into literary canons) becomes accepted and incontrovertible over time. We can highlight the educational canons and their shortcomings, and we can also, as teacher educators, include matter-of-factly items that represent the realities of the student body our education systems now serve.

Embedded Inequalities Remain

In the context of teacher education (Bhopal & Rhamie, 2014), and higher education more broadly (Roth & Ritter, 2021), structural inequalities are deeply embedded in the production of white and settler colonial discourses (Esson, 2020; McKittrick, 2021; Patel, 2014). We are back to the social formation of canons of knowledge: social reproduction means that things are slow to change, and although they may evolve without deliberate impetus, if we wait for the 'passive revolution' (Gramsci, 1971) institutional inertia (Elliott, 2017) and lack of the financial resource to support drastic school-based change will keep us waiting a long time.

Across Commonwealth countries the historical development of schools and curricula was under the British Empire to consolidate and underpin British rule (Kenway et al., 2017). Raffles, writing his *Minute on the Establishment of a Malay College at Singapore* in 1819, wrote of education as a means of providing the 'light of knowledge' as part of the 'benefits of civilisation' wherever a British flag flew around the world (1819, p. 14). Sir John Robert Seeley, a political essayist and professor of history at Cambridge, wrote of his concern for the 'cultivated men' of the Empire (i.e. the Englishmen abroad) who would be living 'in the midst of a vast half-barbarous population' and therefore the need for education to 'enlarge' the views of that population (1870, p. 240). One of the results of the simultaneous rise of education systems with British rule is the embedding of settler colonial attitudes into those education systems. For example, Sriprakash, Rudolph and Gerrard's (2021) analysis *Learning Whiteness* on settler colonialism in the case of Australia. They argue that education (in particular ways in Australia but also more broadly) perpetuates and upholds relations of whiteness across material, epistemic and affective dimensions. Empire left whiteness as a false representation of the universal:

> It is useless to pretend that Dickens 'spoke the language of humanity' or that while male authors can articulate other experiences unaffected by their positionality. The effect of the white curriculum is such that we have imbued white male writers with the power and authority to speak for everyone; marginalised students often find themselves grasping at texts that were not written for them in an attempt to find a shared humanity that is based on their exclusion. (Olufemi, 2019, pp. 57–8)

Even where knowledge originates with non-European sources, white Europeans have tended to adopt, appropriate and claim discoveries for their own or other white Europeans. James Propp (2021), a professor of mathematics in the United States, gives an account on his blog of why labelling the sequence 1, 1, 2, 3, 5, 8, 13, 21 . . . the 'Fibonacci' sequence is failing to give credit to at least two earlier Indian describers of the sequence. He argues that mathematics is already global and diverse in its reference, but that it has a naming problem – not just the names attached to imaginary people in textbooks!

Ahmed (2017) notes the dangers of conflating the history of ideas with white men, and in doing so notes that 'we are being taught where ideas are assumed to originate' (p. 16). A study of Google Scholar's citation data in 2016 revealed only one woman author within the top twenty-five cited books in social sciences – Jean Lave (Green, 2016). The conflation of the history of ideas with white men, allegedly on the basis of chronology, erases those who do not match the archetype. In Michael Hames-García's chapter 'Queer Theory Revisited' in the *Gay Latino Studies Reader* (2011) he demonstrates that the white theorists generally cited on gender and sexuality actually come after theorists of colour, and chronology is largely ignored in favour of white people citing white people (and leaving race out of the intersectional discussion). White citation practices persist: Smith and Garrett-Scott (2021) demonstrate the systematic under-citation of Black women anthropologists relative to their contribution to the field, and particularly in top-tier journals where in the rare instances they are cited, they are cited by other Black anthropologists. More broadly, topics which have been part of Indigenous discourse and intellectual traditions from years can suddenly be 'discovered' by Western scholars without acknowledgement of those discourses. Zoe Todd, a Métis scholar, tells the story of going to hear 'the Great Latour' (2016, p. 6) talk about climate, in the hope of seeing Indigenous thinking given credit, but slowly losing that hope.

Again, I thought with a sinking feeling in my chest, it appeared that another Euro-Western academic narrative . . . was spinning itself on the backs of non-European thinkers . . . here we were celebrating and worshipping a European thinker for 'discovering', or newly articulating by drawing on a European intellectual heritage, what many an Indigenous thinker around the world could have told you for millennia: the climate is a common organizing force! (Todd, 2016, p. 7)

Such is the risk of conflating the history of ideas with white men: missing those who have gone before, and missing their insights.

A number of programmes for Initial Teacher Education in post-colonial or Global South contexts are taking deliberate steps to incorporate more local traditions of knowledge or to challenge embedded inequalities in academic disciplines. Formabiap, for example, an Indigenous-led teacher education programme in the Peruvian Amazon, has a focus on the ontological and epistemological aspects of intercultural knowledge exchanges, utilizing community mentors as 'sages' to embed a 'dialogue of knowledge' framework between Indigenous and Western knowledges (Rivera et al., 2023). In doing so, they admit a wider frame from which valid knowledge can come, than that which is typically legitimized within the Western academy. Indigenous epistemologies allow that 'dreams, visions, vision quests, and interactions with nature, along with insight and intuition are all salient to meaning and knowledge' (Welch, 2019, p. 63). Another Initial Teacher Education project engaged students on programmes to become primary educators with precolonial Indigenous heritage in the Canary Islands and Mexico, enabling them to critique primary textbooks through considering the juxtaposition of the European colonial/monumental heritage with the Indigenous non-monumental heritage (Farrujia de la Rosa et al., 2023). Deliberately placing pre and (post) colonial adjacent to each other, or Indigenous and Western knowledges, provides a structure for highlighting inequal power structures in knowledge and provoking discussion and consideration on the part of individual teachers or future teachers.

Indeed, combatting these embedded inequalities requires a great deal of effort on the part of the individual teacher to ensure that they are not simply reproducing knowledge from their own schooldays, but are engaging with different material. As well as race and gender, we need to think about the knowledge of and representation of disability within our classrooms (e.g. Jacobson & Bialka, 2023), and the representation and recognition of working-class people and those who live in poverty as well as the middle-class examples who are assumed to be the desired endpoint of a successful education. We also have the ability to use new understandings of life to engage with old material. In classics education Rabinowitz and McHardy (2014) address a number of topics, common in Latin and Greek writings, that are difficult to discuss and which students may have had experience of in their own lives – including slavery, infanticide, abortion, rape and domestic violence – developing a sensitive pedagogy for handling this material. Similarly, the new beginners' Latin textbook *Suburani* (Hands Up Education, 2020) has been developed with a diverse and inclusive representation of the Roman Empire in mind, including using the preferred term 'enslaved person' to translate *servus* in deference to modern discourses on slavery.

Challenging these embedded inequalities is important because they damage the very students that we are supposed to be supporting into life success. The concept of 'recognition' comes from Canadian multiculturalism:

> The thesis is that our identity is partly shaped by recognitions or its absence, often by the *mis*recognition of others, and so a person or group of people can suffer real damage, real distortion if the people or society around them mirror back to them a confining or demeaning or contemptible picture of themselves. Nonrecognition or misrecognition can inflict

harm, can be a form of oppression, imprisoning someone in a false, distorted, and reduced mode of being. (Taylor, 1994, p. 25)

Curriculum is an important aspect of recognition, misrecognition and absence in terms of societal representation of different groups of people, and so is the educational theory or disciplinary theory that we use to provide the background to our teaching.

A greater realization of the value of Indigenous knowledges has been seen across the world, in a variety of contexts, but particularly in relation to managing risk and challenge in relation to climate change, as for example in community-led projects in China (Wang et al., 2019) and Nigeria (Mairiga & Ibrahim, 2021). The greater emphasis on relational knowing in many Indigenous cultures (as opposed to human-centred worldviews) (Mika, 2017) is especially apt for thinking about future solutions to climate change. The *Coolangatta Statement on Indigenous Peoples' Rights in Education* (Morgan et al., 1999) articulated a rights-based agenda for Indigenous people in education which has been somewhat taken up in legislation in Australia and New Zealand. Teaching history in settler colony countries often requires the memory-based oral stories of Indigenous peoples that are not represented in the history books to balance out settler histories that serve to erase the original residents of an area (see MacDonald & Kidman, 2022, for an example of this approach in New Zealand). Education, and indeed the school, has become 'an influential setting in which these differing world views have the opportunity to rub up against each other' (Vass & Hogarth, 2022, p. 4).

A Curriculum for All

One of the (slightly) more hidden aspects when considering knowledge for all is the structures of education systems themselves. The recent pandemic highlighted the greater challenges faced by both students and teachers from disadvantaged backgrounds. Socio-economic background influences future educational choices, such as which schools to go to, whether to go to university as well as which university. This leads to those from more advantaged backgrounds being overrepresented in particular types of school (e.g. grammar schools in the UK or charter schools in the United States, universities and types of university, resulting in a perception that these schools are better and that a university education has more societal value over a vocational route. This valuing is also visible within curricula at several points during someone's educational experiences, through the time allocated to different subjects, through the choices (or not) around what to study, through the gatekeeping subjects for further study or employment. The high value placed on mathematics is also evident in research analysing the earnings of people aged thirty-four in England who had studied a range of subjects at A level: mathematics was the only subject with a wage premium (Adkins & Noyes, 2016).

One of the premises behind the development of a national curriculum in the UK was to outline the knowledge or content that all students should experience in school. Yet until recently there were two tiers of examinations at aged sixteen in England, where students with a history of lower prior attainment were grouped into classes that then experienced a narrower curriculum. This sorting of students into groups according to their prior attainment, however, has no overall effect on their later performance, but it does significantly contribute to exacerbating educational inequalities (Terrin & Triventi, 2022). This practice of grouping students, either through their choices of schools (e.g. grammar vs secondary modern, vocational vs academic) or through streaming, tracking, setting or ability grouping of some kind is common in many countries. The arguments supporting this type of grouping is that teaching can be adapted to the students' abilities, interests and needs. Yet it is well established that these groupings are strongly influenced by economic, social and cultural factors, where students with a higher socio-economic background with the same attainment than a more disadvantaged peer are more likely to be in a higher set or in a selective school.

The ambition of working towards knowledge for all involves addressing multiple challenges including complex, robust and critical engagements with academic disciplines and their relationships with school subjects; embedded inequities; structural issues around formal education, and more. Not underestimating the scale of this challenge, we sketch out a number of ways forward in the next and final chapter: 'Consequences for Practice'.

CHAPTER 7

Consequences for Practice

This chapter locates the discussions across the rest of the book firmly in the realm of teacher education practice. We begin by arguing for an expansion of the knowledges which are given attention in teacher education, and grounding that attention throughout the initial teacher education curriculum. We encourage readers – and all teachers – to reflect critically on the kinds of knowledge they value. Teacher educators need to support this critical reflection in order to enable teachers to critically engage with debates on knowledge and skills, and rhetoric around both, throughout their careers. The structural realities of teachers' and teacher educators' practice in some parts of the world (e.g. some US states and England) – particularly surrounding policy that prohibits certain knowledges from being taught – makes the need for this criticality timely (Marrun et al., 2023; Wyse & Bradbury, 2022). Another consequence of the more expansive conception of knowledge that we have argued for – and which is also in tension with prohibitions of certain knowledges – is a need to embrace a greater level of complexity about knowledge. We reflect on implications of disciplinary knowledge epistemologies for the development of educational/social scientific epistemologies and the potential consequences for teachers and teacher educators. We end by considering the potential of teacher education and teachers' ongoing engagement with their own education for the creation of new knowledges (knowledge for teaching, knowledge in action, etc.) in each moment in the classroom, and more broadly within the discipline, by thinking about the implications for research.

What Knowledges Should We Be Thinking About in Teacher Education?

Teacher education programmes have a very short space of time in which to provide a grounding for the whole careers of teachers, and there is both a demand and a need for concentration on practical issues such as behaviour management and planning skills.

Beyond this kind of practical knowledge, typically two knowledges get the most attention in teacher education: subject knowledge and what is often termed pedagogical content knowledge. That is to say, what content knowledge do you have, and do you know how to teach it?

We would like to suggest that teacher education should bring in a much broader range of knowledges and ensure engagement with them. It is important, for example, that teachers should have a sufficient grounding in the debates around knowledge-rich curricula, cultural capital, powerful knowledge and so on to be able to understand and contribute to discussion around the purposes, ways and means of education. This is the essential critical literacy that our profession needs in order to maintain our autonomy. To take one example in the English context, government policy has mandated the use of phonics for teaching reading, publishing official core criteria for systematic synthetic phonics (SSP), teaching programmes and controlling a validation process for these programmes (DfE, 2023a). The 'reading framework' (DfE, 2023b) repeats the authorized account of SSP for initial teacher education, citing the DfE's early career framework which 'sets out the expectation that all early career teachers learn about phonics and says that SSP is the most effective approach for teaching pupils to decode' (p. 6). The main accountability lever used to enforce the prohibition of alternative knowledges is through the inspectorate Ofsted, whose 2023 inspection framework includes the following in the description of a 'Good' provider (bold added):

> training ensures that trainees learn to teach early reading using systematic synthetic phonics, as outlined in the ITT core content framework, and that **trainees are not taught to teach competing approaches to early reading.**

Whereas, a provider receiving the lowest judgement (Inadequate: 4) states the opposite; that trainees have not been restricted from learning about alternatives: 'training does not ensure that trainees only learn to teach decoding using systematic synthetic phonics as part of early reading.' The wider principle of government-sanction and prohibited knowledges presents challenges for teachers and teacher educators, particularly when the tensions between these prohibitions and academic freedom are so apparent. The specific example of teaching reading is also problematic because of the differences between the research evidence and government-sanctioned summaries of this evidence. In Wyse and Bradbury's (2022) terms, the 'most robust research evidence, from randomised control trials with longitudinal designs, shows that the approach to phonics and reading teaching in England is not sufficiently underpinned by research evidence' (p. 1).

We also need to draw the attention of future teachers to the ways in which misinformation and disinformation spread, not only for their own benefit but also in order that they can equip their students with this empowering knowledge. Ultimately, teacher education needs to be not only about knowledge of education, but also about how that knowledge is formed, and evidenced, and how we as individuals respond. Teacher educators are preparing student teachers for a long-term professional life, not just the first few years of teaching, although that is something that we often have to fight for. Knowledge does not stand still, and providing the base for life-long learning is important – especially if part of that is supporting the development of epistemological worlds views to understand past, present and future shifts in knowledge. The highly politicized example of critical race theory (CRT) in the United States, and mis/dis-information around race and racism are a focal point for 'escalating state licensure regulations as well as state and federal policy mandates' (Lees et al., 2023, p. 2). Lee et al.'s systematic review of literature on teacher education highlights the challenges that these structural issues pose for individuals trying to expand the knowledges to which teachers are introduced: 'there are many restrictions to bringing such commitments to fruition, especially through isolated efforts by single faculty' (p. 9). Understanding something of the political economy of teaching and teacher education – knowledge about knowledge and the structures within which it is produced and legitimated (or silenced) – is a necessary aspect of teacher preparation.

Beyond these knowledges about knowledge itself, we have argued that teachers need knowledge of social inequalities in order to enable them to become agents of change, in keeping with the idea of teaching as a vocation and the rhetoric of social justice which underpins many current debates. There is some evidence that encouraging beginning teachers to adopt a research orientation towards these kinds of topics is an effective way of promoting their knowledge and understanding (Burn et al., 2016). Developing knowledge about educational research more generally, how it happens, what criteria to judge it by and its role in teaching is also becoming a more fundamental part of teacher education.

Similar underlying critical concerns also support teacher education's role in embedding knowledge for all. By ensuring that beginning teachers understand the processes through which subject canons are formed, that is, critically evaluating whose knowledge is included – and whose is excluded – teacher educators can help to challenge the unknowing reproduction of social inequalities as represented in the curriculum. The promotion of a broader range of knowledges has further consequences for teacher education and for teachers themselves. In the study of literature, for example, in order to teach texts by authors of colour, we need to know not only what texts exist, but also which of those texts support the kinds of learning we want to promote at a given stage, which ones are accessible, and ultimately be confident that we can pull from them appropriate interpretations, in collaboration with our students. This may mean a certain amount of exploratory reading carried out in the teacher's own time, since few have the grounding needed for such a venture from their own education (Elliott et al., 2021). It also puts the onus on teacher educators to model the range of knowledge that we want to see being demonstrated in the classroom; to continue with literature as an example, it means using unfamiliar texts with beginning teachers to teach planning. Teacher educators have the opportunity to shape practice on a wide scale, via their influence on beginning teachers, mentors and the departments in which student teachers are placed. Setting a task to produce resources which reflect a more inclusive vision of the world during college time can create ripples in the pond of practice as time-strapped teachers snap up ready-made materials from their trainees. Equally, most courses will set some kind of knowledge development target during the period of studying to teach, and these can and should be used to broaden student teachers' views of their subjects.

Problematizing the Nature of Knowledge

One of the things we have tried to do throughout this book is to show that knowledge is not a simple thing: as a keyword in Williams' sense it is inherently contested and subject to the interests, priorities and energy that people bring to it. Focusing on 'knowledge-based' education could mean many things, including across different subjects and phases of education. In problematizing the nature of knowledge, we are not simply trying to complicate things for the sake of it. There are particular consequences for teachers. First, as we demonstrated in Chapter 2, students in school bounce between different disciplinary approaches to knowledge throughout the day. Because 'knowing' is different in different subjects, and what counts as evidence for knowledge differs too, tasks at the beginning of lessons can be important scaffolds for students to transition between ways of thinking.

Second, problematizing the nature of knowledge means that it is important for teachers to think about the consequences for cognitive science approaches such as retrieval practice within their own subject. What counts as the kind of valuable knowledge that you want students to have embedded in their long-term memory? This is not to say that no low-level factual recall is useful – in science the labelling of parts, or in modern languages giving vocabulary a certain level of automaticity are each useful. Despite the derision that it sometimes attracts, knowing continents, countries and capitals is useful for geography. But if this is the only type of knowledge whose retrieval is being practised, then students are not getting the most benefit from the approach but are only being offered narrowed versions of the rich subject traditions and knowledges that they otherwise might be introduced to.

In addition, the types and nature of assessment used in schools and across educational jurisdictions (whether those are states or countries – or beyond) produces 'washback' into curricula and classrooms across the world. Assessment types produce the ways we conceptualize and teach knowledge in schools, and the ways that pupils understand knowledge. The example of the Harvard entrance test creating the secondary literary curriculum we gave in Chapter 6 is a good demonstration of the ways in which tests can have unexpected – and lasting – consequences. More recently, AP curricula in the United States ('Advanced Placement' courses taken by advanced high school students for college credits), whether AP African American Studies in 2023 or AP history in 2014, have been rewritten to accommodate political direction. By reducing to non-examined status certain topics, or eliminating certain terms altogether, the assessment drives the terms of engagement with knowledge in classrooms across the United States.

To follow Spiderman, with great power comes great responsibility, and thus those who set the specifications for national or state examinations should consider carefully what the curriculum they are promoting looks like. Whose knowledge is being promoted, and whose knowledge is being valued? This is just as true for teacher education curricula, which may be closely mandated as with some state standards in the United States, or the Core Curriculum Framework in England, or more flexibly aligned with professional judgement, and the interrelation between research and practice, as in Norway (Cochran-Smith et al., 2020).

While few of us have much influence on the large-scale assessments that differentiate between students on a national basis for the purposes of university entrance or gateway qualifications, we do have the ability to think about what we are doing in our classrooms and institutions. What gets measured comes to matter. If we test low-level factual knowledge, that becomes the version of our subject that students value. This has consequences for 'validity' of educational assessment – the extent to which we are assessing what we purport to assess. One way around this is to invoke 'authentic assessment', a concept which seems to have originated with Newmann and Archbold who argue that 'the quality and utility of assessment rest upon the extent to which the outcomes measured represent appropriate, meaningful, significant, and worthwhile forms of human accomplishment' (1992, p. 71), which they synthesize as 'authenticity'. The challenge of ensuring that your classroom assessment is a 'significant and worthwhile' accomplishment for your students is no small one, but paying attention to the nature of the knowledge you are expecting them to display is one way.

Fundamentally, by making 'knowledge' the subject of challenge we are returning to the most important question in any lesson: What is it that I want the students to learn? Is it about *this* rock face, or is it about how to examine and understand any rock face? Is it the themes of *this* poem or how to analyse any poem? Is it how to do *this* sum or is it how to extrapolate from this sum to a range of others? Are we teaching students how to do mathematics, or how to think like mathematicians? To do physics or to think like physicists? To speak French or to think like linguists? (Sometimes the answer is both.)

Implications – Instructor, Facilitator, Explainer, Director, Deliverer, Provocateur

Conceptualizing knowledge in more complex ways also requires us to think about how we conceptualize the role of the teacher in the classroom. A knowledge-rich approach is often found in tandem with direct instruction (little 'di' as opposed to the formalized scripted approach of Direct Instruction in the Engelmann-Becker tradition (Englemann & Colvin, 2006)). A conception of knowledge as being simple, fixed, information meshes happily with a delivery approach, whereby the teacher speaks and the student learns. However, where we begin to think about knowledge as being constructed between people or discursively, as in English, we see that such a delivery approach is not appropriate. Indeed, Burgess, Rawal and Taylor (2022), analysing around 14,000 GCSE results from thirty-two schools in search of effective teaching, found that the most effective thing an English teacher could do was facilitate discussion and interaction among their class in terms of raising attainment. This is not true of all subjects, however: in mathematics individual practice was more important, supporting our arguments that knowledge, what counts as knowledge and how we acquire it varies between subjects and disciplines. A complex understanding of knowledge means that teachers may have to move between roles in the classroom: there is a role for delivery of content, but it must also be explained (and clear, unambiguous explanation is the key feature of Direct Instruction in the Engelmann-Becker tradition). We might be facilitating discussion, or we might be acting as provocateurs in order to challenge students' instinctive answers and getting them to do the explaining.

Having said that, we also know that the curriculum creates a framing effect on the way that we see knowledge in schools. Curricula create artificial distinctions between different subjects – so, for example, dividing mathematics from science and then within mathematics making the distinction between algebra versus geometry, and so on. This affects the ways that students build mental schema of knowledge, and can prevent them from making connections between what they have learned in different subject classrooms, hindering the kinds of synthesis can that make learning more efficient or lead to creative realizations. Teachers can and should highlight connections in the classroom by identifying underlying patterns that hold true beneath subjects. In both English and history, for example, analysing texts (or 'sources') can benefit from thinking about the audience they were composed for and how that might affect how they are written. In both grammar teaching and mathematics we might need to think as teachers whether we wait until students have an understanding of a concept before we give them the name by which to label it, or if we start with the definition and then move to the examples. Across subjects, but particularly in mathematics and the sciences, the principles of the specific and the general – the example and what is it an example of? – are key to the development of abstraction as a process and the epistemological assumptions underpinning it.

In Chapter 2 we considered the relation between existing epistemological world views, particularly those which are attributable to disciplinary epistemologies, and the epistemological world views that teachers bring to education and educational research. Disciplinary epistemologies can have consequences for teachers teaching out of subject, in terms of how comfortable they are with the material and the teaching methods adopted in that subject. Understanding your own and others epistemological world views can also be important for uncovering some fundamental misunderstandings in learning, or understanding why certain educators resist educational research.

For many the 'gold standard' of research is the large-scale quantitative research that which comes out of a positivist, cause-and-effect paradigm, modelled after the experimental hard sciences (Lortie-Forgues & Inglis, 2019; Ginsburg & Smith, 2016). In recent decades, the United States and the UK have seen an emphasis on the Randomised Control Trial (RCT) as the most valued method for educational research, adopted by analogy with medical research, and promoted by government sources, such as the report *Building Evidence into Education* (Goldacre, 2013). It is easy to see that those whose epistemologies emphasize the role of the individual and context in the construction of knowledge might resist the lessons pushed from such methodologies. If we draw on the cognitive heuristics and biases model of thinking, the 'availability' heuristic (Kahneman, 2011) means that humans are greatly influenced by the example which comes easily to mind: and if your classroom experience contradicts the research, then that is a powerful push for many epistemological world views.

It is also important for teacher educators to acknowledge the variety of epistemological world views that their student teachers may encounter in the classroom. In particular, the relational epistemologies of Indigenous peoples have not been given due consideration in the educational and academic establishment to date (Tuhiwai Smith, 2021; Patel, 2016). Relational epistemologies consider people as part of a network of relations and connections. 'They have connections with the living and the nonliving, with land, with the earth, with animals, and with other beings. There is an emphasis on an I/we relationship as opposed to the Western I/ you relationship with its emphasis on the individual' (Chilisa, 2019, p. 24). This collective paradigm is also prominent in many Asian cultures (e.g. Yang et al., 2022; Mori & Davies, 2015). Respecting and understanding the variety of epistemologies that different cultural backgrounds can bring to the classroom is a crucial way of creating an inclusive educational environment which does not alienate students and supports them in achieving.

Implications for Research

Through our discussion of knowledge in teacher education we have raised a wide range of questions about policy, practice, discourse and research, which we draw together here under the themes of: knowledge, information, skills and Google; teacher knowledge; subjects, disciplines and knowledge; power and knowledge; and knowledge for all. We have used a holder for [the subject] as a way to refer either/both to school subjects (such as mathematics, English or geography), or to teacher education itself: knowledge, information, skills and Google:

- What is the nature of the information handling skills taught through the [subject area] curriculum?

- In what ways might 'lateral reading' be used in [subject area], and what are the challenges to doing this?

- What are the implications of using retrieval practice for students' conceptions of [the subject]? Which aspects of the subject (e.g. terminology, concepts, theories) are prioritized and which are side-lined through retrieval quizzes?

- How are 'information' and 'knowledge' used in [subject area], in what ways do these meanings vary across international contexts, and what are the implications of these different discourses?

- To what extent can subject-specific approaches to mistakes, errors and misconceptions be productively shared and used in whole-school cultures?

Teacher knowledge:

- In what ways does subject knowledge in [subject area] differ between the school subject and academic discipline?

- What spaces does knowledge travel through as it moves into the classroom? What actors work in these spaces? In what ways is knowledge reconfigured along these journeys?

- How does the structure of subject matter of [subject area] vary between subjects, and what are the implications for teacher education programmes?

- What knowledge do teachers in [subject area] need? In what ways do these needs vary across subjects and international contexts?

Subjects, disciplines and knowledge:

- What different epistemologies do students encounter through their days in school?

- How might teacher educators prepare teachers for anticipating and dealing with students' encounters with different epistemologies?

- What are the main points of tension (in terms of assumptions about and use of knowledge) between different subject areas?

- In what ways does and should teachers' presentation of knowledge (particularly as fixed/dynamic, certain/uncertain) change across phases of education?

- What is the relationship between enabling students to become familiar with *doing* the [subject area] and knowing things about [subject area]?

- How might interdisciplinary collaborations around models, theories and concepts produce new insights for cross-curricular teaching?

- How are teacher explanations commented on in lesson observation feedback? What are the features of 'good' explanations, and how do they vary across subject areas?

Power and knowledge:

- How has [subject area] been shaped and driven by aspects of 'shadow'? In what ways are these areas of 'shadow' being addressed, and what are the possible implications for teacher education?

- What are the dominant narratives about [subject area], and to what extent do they engage with both 'shadow' and 'shine'?

- What happens if we start our understandings of [subject area] from the Global South?

- What kinds of insights have powerful knowledge discourses made possible in [subject area]?

- What are the limitations of powerful knowledge as a concept for research in [subject area]?

- In what ways does the idea of disciplinary literacy apply to [subject area]?

Knowledge for all:

- Who, and what groups, are represented in the [subject area] curriculum? Who are not?

- What narratives does the [subject area] curriculum construct about different peoples and places?

- What new stories should teacher education be telling about knowledge, its nature and its role in education?

- How can teacher education balance critique of reductionist accounts of knowledge against positive arguments for the importance of knowledge properly understood?

- What might we learn from previous curricular shifts for research and practice in teacher education?

- In what ways might past curricular shifts illuminate contemporary opportunities and challenges for constructing curriculum that are diverse, inclusive and accessible for all?

- How are [subject area's] curriculum priorities related to and shaped by global policy networks and discourses?

- What should teacher education prioritize in order to contribute to more just, equitable and inclusive futures?

- How can international collaborations most effectively support colleagues operating in systems prohibiting certain kinds of knowledges?

- How might policymakers engage with a richer diversity of knowledges?

What should be prioritized in collaborative efforts to critically engage with structural challenges facing teachers and teacher educators?

An enduring theme of these questions, and of our discussion, is that our grasp of knowledge is partial, limited, situated and yet generative. Constructing new knowledge is exciting in the way it makes visible new horizons and opens new possibilities. With these new possibilities come new questions that will lead to new insights, new understandings and new knowledges. Questions about knowledge are deeply connected to the wealth of philosophical discussion about epistemology that now stretches over thousands of years, touching on the most basic concerns about what it is to be human, how we might best come to know and what we ought to do with that knowledge. The distinctive context of teacher education, and teacher education in this day and age, applies these more fundamental philosophical questions to a period in which increasingly powerful technologies shape the circulation and accessibility of information in radically new ways. The canon of accepted knowledge through which new information is viewed has been shown to be far from neutral, as racialized, classed and gendered inequalities are reflected and refracted through the knowledges – including knowledges produced through academic disciplines. Giving all young people access to the riches of disciplinary ways of knowing is an important part of formal education, and teacher education has a key role to play at the interface between academic disciplines and school subjects. But this relationship is not simple or obvious, and we have revisited analyses of the shadow and shine of disciplinary knowledges to argue that there are ongoing questions that need to be asked about the ways in which disciplines reproduce narrow, partial and unequal understandings. A more complex understanding of disciplinary literacies that moves us beyond the limitations of a 'powerful knowledge' binary also, we hope, generates a suite of questions to be explored through teacher education that will equip and empower teacher educators and teachers to make knowledge accessible to all. We hope the questions offered earlier might offer a useful stimulus for further research at a range of scales from individual practitioner studies to larger scale international comparative and longitudinal work.

REFERENCES

Adkins, M., & Noyes, A. (2016). Reassessing the economic value of advanced level mathematics. *British Educational Research Journal*, 42(1), 93–116. https://doi.org/10.1002/berj.3219

Adoniou, M. (2015). Teacher knowledge: A complex tapestry. *Asia-Pacific Journal of Teacher Education*, 43(2), 99–116. https://doi.org/10.1080/1359866X.2014.932330

Ahmed, S. (2017). *Living a feminist life*. Duke University Press.

Amoore, L. (2020). *Cloud ethics: Algorithms and the attributes of ourselves and others*. Duke University Press.

AQA (2018). *GCSE English literature hub schools network meeting presentation slides*. https://filestore.aqa.org.uk/resources/english/AQA-GCSE-ENG-HUB-AUT-2018-SLIDES.PDF

Arner, D. G. (1972). *Perception, reason, and knowledge: An introduction to epistemology*. Scott, Foresman and Co.

Backman, E., & Barker, D. M. (2020). Re-thinking pedagogical content knowledge for physical education teachers–implications for physical education teacher education. *Physical Education and Sport Pedagogy*, 25(5), 451–63. https://doi.org/10.1080/17408989.2020.1734554

Baird, J.-A., & Elliott, V. (2018). Metrics in education-control and corruption. *Oxford Review of Education*, 44(5), 533–44. https://doi.org/10.1080/03054985.2018.1504858

Ball, S. J. (2016). Following policy: Networks, network ethnography and education policy mobilities. *Journal of Education Policy*, 31(5), 549–66. https://doi.org/10.1080/02680939.2015.1122232

Ball, S. J. (2020). *The 10 books that made me a sociologist of education*. BERA Blog. https://www.bera.ac.uk/blog/the-10-books-that-made-me-a-sociologist-of-education

Barwell, R. (2013). Discursive psychology as an alternative perspective on mathematics teacher knowledge. *ZDM - The*

International Journal on Mathematics Education, *45*(4), 595–606. https://doi.org/10.1007/s11858-013-0508-4

BERA-RSA (2014). *Research and the teaching profession: Building the capacity for a self-improving education system*. https://www.thersa.org/reports/research-and-the-teaching-profession-building-the-capacity-for-a-self-improving-education-system

Bernstein, B. (1999). Vertical and horizontal discourse: An essay. *British Journal of Sociology of Education*, *20*(2), 157–73. https://doi.org/10.1080/01425699995380

Bhopal, K., & Rhamie, J. (2014). Initial teacher training: Understanding 'race,' diversity and inclusion. *Race Ethnicity and Education*, *17*(3), 304–25. https://doi.org/10.1080/13613324.2013.832920

Bitchener, J., & Ferris, D. R. (2012). *Written corrective feedback in second language acquisition and writing*. Routledge. https://doi.org/10.4324/9780203832400

Bloom, H. (1990). *The western canon*. Harcourt Brace and Company.

Borowski, A., Carlson, J., Fischer, H. E., & Henze, I. (2012). Different models and methods to measure teachers' pedagogical content knowledge. In C. Bruguière, A. Tiberghien, & P.Clément (Eds.), *Proceedings of the ESERA 2011 conference: Science learning and citizenship*. European Science Education Research Association.

Bray, W. S. (2011). A collective case study of the influence of teachers' beliefs and knowledge on error-handling practices during class discussion of mathematics. *Journal for Research in Mathematics Education*, *42*(1), 2–38. https://doi.org/10.5951/jresematheduc.42.1.0002

Bray, W. S. (2013). How to leverage the potential of mathematical errors. *Teaching Children Mathematics*, *19*(7), 424–31. https://doi.org/10.5951/teacchilmath.19.7.0424

Breakspear, S. (2014). How does PISA shape education policy making? Why how we measure learning determines what counts in education. *Centre for Strategic Education: Seminar Series*, *240*, 1–16.

Brownlee, J., Schraw, G., & Berthelsen, D. (Eds.). (2011). *Personal epistemology and teacher education*. Routledge.

Bruner, J. S. (1960). *The process of education*. Harvard University Press. https://www.hup.harvard.edu/catalog.php?isbn=9780674710016

Burbules, N. C., & Densmore, K. (1991). The limits of making teaching a profession. *Educational Policy*, 5(1), 44–63. https://doi.org/10.1177/0895904891005001004

Burgess, S., Rawal, S., & Taylor, E. S. (2022). *Characterising effective teaching*. Nuffield Foundation.

Burn, K., Conway, R., Edwards, A., & Harries, E. (2021). The role of school-based research champions in a school–university partnership. *British Educational Research Journal*, 47(3), 616–33. https://doi.org/10.1002/berj.3675

Burn, K., Mutton, T., & Thompson, I. (2022). *Practical theorising in teacher education: Holding theory and practice together*. Routledge. https://doi.org/10.4324/9781003183945

Burn, K., Mutton, T., Thompson, I., Ingram, J., McNicholl, J., & Firth, R. (2016). The impact of adopting a research orientation towards use of the Pupil Premium Grant in preparing beginning teachers in England to understand and work effectively with young people living in poverty. *Journal of Education for Teaching*, 42(4). https://doi.org/10.1080/02607476.2016.1215551

Burton, L. (2004). *Mathematicians as enquirers: Learning about learning mathematics*. Kluwer Academic Publishers.

Canpolat, N., Pinarbasi, T., & Sözbilir, M. (2006). Prospective teachers' misconceptions of vaporization and vapor pressure. *Journal of Chemical Education*, 83(8), 1237–42. https://doi.org/10.1021/ed083p1237

Castree, N. (2014). *Making sense of nature: Representation, politics and democracy*. Routledge.

Catling, S., & Martin, F. (2011). Contesting powerful knowledge: The primary geography curriculum as an articulation between academic and children's (ethno-) geographies. *Curriculum Journal*, 22(3), 317–35. https://doi.org/10.1080/09585176.2011.601624

Chakrabarty, D. (2000). *Provincializing Europe: Postcolonial thought and historical difference*. Princeton University Press. https://doi.org/10.2307/2692957

Chantiluke, R., Kwoba, B., & Nkopo, A. (Eds.). (2018). *Rhodes must fall: The struggle to decolonise the racist heart of empire*. Bloomsbury Academic.

Chilisa, B. (2019). *Indigenous research methodologies*. Sage Publications.

Chipeniuk, R. (1998). Lay theories of spring: Displacement of common-sense understandings of nature by 'expert' ideas. *International Research in Geographical and Environmental Education, 7*(1), 14–25. https://doi.org/10.1080/10382049808667555

Clarke, D., & Hollingsworth, H. (2002). Elaborating a model of teacher professional growth. *Teaching and Teacher Education, 18*, 947–67. https://doi.org/10.1016/s0742-051x(02)00053-7

Cochran, K. F., DeRuiter, J. A., & King, R. A. (1993). Pedagogical content knowing: An integrative model for teacher preparation. *Journal of Teacher Education, 44*(4), 263–72. https://doi.org/10.1177/0022487193044004004

Cochran-Smith, M., Alexandersson, M., Oancea, A., Hammerness, K., Ellis, V., Grudnoff, L., & Toom,A. (2020). *Transforming Norwegian teacher education: The final report of the international advisory panel for primary and lower secondary teacher education.* NOKUT.https://www.nokut.no/globalassets/nokut/rapporter/ua/2020/transforming-norwegian-teacher-education-2020.pdf

Cochran-Smith, M., & Lytle, S. L. (1999). Relationships of knowledge and practice: Teacher learning in communities. *Review of Research in Education, 24*(1), 249–305. https://doi.org/10.3102/0091732X024001249

Connell, R. (2007). *Southern theory: Social science and the global dynamics of knowledge.* Wiley.

Copur-Gencturk, Y., Plowman, D., & Bai, H. (2019). Mathematics teachers' learning: Identifying key learning opportunities linked to teachers' knowledge growth. *American Educational Research Journal, 56*(5), 1590–628. https://doi.org/10.3102/0002831218820033

Craske, J. (2021). Logics, rhetoric and 'the blob': Populist logic in the conservative reforms to English schooling. *British Educational Research Journal, 47*(2), 279–98. https://doi.org/10.1002/berj.3682

Cultural Capital | Social Theory Rewired (n.d.). *2016.* Retrieved 19 September 2022, from https://routledgesoc.com/category/profile-tags/cultural-capital

Cuoco, A., Paul Goldenberg, E., & Mark, J. (1996). Habits of mind: An organizing principle for mathematics curricula. *The Journal of Mathematical Behavior, 15*(4), 375–402. https://doi.org/10.1016/S0732-3123(96)90023-1

Cushing, I., & Snell, J. (2022). The (white) ears of ofsted: A raciolinguistic perspective on the listening practices of the schools inspectorate. *Language in Society*, 1–24. https://doi.org/10.1017/S0047404522000094

Daniels, H. (Ed.). (2015). *Introduction to vygotsky*. Routledge.

Delpit, L. (2011). The silenced dialogue: Power and pedagogy in educating other people's children. *Harvard Educational Review*, *58*(3), 280–99. https://doi.org/10.17763/haer.58.3.c43481778r528qw4

Department for Education (2011). *The framework for the national curriculum: A report by the expert panel for the national curriculum review*. Available at https://assets.publishing.service.gov.uk/media/5a7572c5ed915d6faf2b3104/NCR-Expert_Panel_Report.pdf

Department for Education (2023a). Choosing a phonics teaching programme. Retrieved 10 October 2023, from https://www.gov.uk/government/publications/choosing-a-phonics-teaching-programme/list-of-phonics-teaching-programmes

Department for Education (2023b). *The reading framework*. Retrieved 10 October 2023, from https://assets.publishing.service.gov.uk/government/uploads/system/uploads/attachment_data/file/1186732/The_reading_framework.pdf

Dickens, C. (1854). *Hard times*. Open Road Media. http://ebookcentral.proquest.com/lib/oxford/detail.action?docID=1986607

Donaldson, M. L. (1986). *Children's explanations: A psycholinguistic study*. Cambridge University Press.

Driver, F. (2013). Hidden histories made visible? Reflections on a geographical exhibition. *Transactions of the Institute of British Geographers*, *38*(3), 420–35. https://doi.org/10.1111/J.1475-5661.2012.00529.X

Dutant, J. (2015). The legend of the justified true belief analysis. *Philosophical Perspectives*, *29*(1), 95–145. https://doi.org/10.1111/PHPE.12061

Elliott, V. (2017). Gender and the contemporary educational canon in the UK. *International Journal of English Studies*, *17*(2), 45–62. https://doi.org/10.6018/ijes/2017/2/264251

Elliott, V. (2020). *Knowledge in English: Canon, curriculum and cultural literacy*. Routledge.

Elliott, V. (2022). *Foundations of educational research*. Bloomsbury Academic.

Elliott, V., Nelson-Addy, L., Chantiluke, R., & Courtney, M. (2021). *Lit in colour: Diversity in literature in English schools*. Penguin & Runnymede Trust.

Ellis, V. (2007). *Subject knowledge and teacher education: The development of beginning teachers' thinking*. Continuum. https://www.bloomsbury.com/uk/subject-knowledge-and-teacher -education-9781441119018/

Englemann, S., & Colvin, G. (2006). *Rubric for identifying authentic direct instruction programs*. Engelmann Foundation.

Ernest, P. (1989). Philosophy, mathematics and education. *International Journal of Mathematical Education in Science and Technology*, *20*(4), 555–9. https://doi.org/10.1080 /0020739890200409

Esson, J. (2020). 'The why and the white': Racism and curriculum reform in British geography. *Area*, *52*(4), 708–15. https://doi.org /10.1111/AREA.12475

Esson, J., & Last, A. (2020). Anti-racist learning and teaching in British geography. *Area*, *52*(4), 668–77. https://doi.org/10.1111/ area.12658

Evening Standard (2022, March 23). *Clampdown on 'Mickey Mouse' degrees in major funding overhall*. https://www.standard .co.uk/news/education/universities-degrees-higher-education -grades-funding-student-loans-b984218.html

Fargher, M., Mitchell, D., & Till, E. (Eds.). (2021). *Recontextualising geography in education*. Springer International Publishing. https:// doi.org/10.1007/978-3-030-73722-1

Farrujia de la Rosa, A. J., Ritchie, P. S. H., & Martínez, T. E. Z. (2023). Indigenous heritage as an educational resource in primary education. *Oxford Review of Education*, *49*(4), 446–60.

Felbrich, A., Kaiser, G., & Schmotz, C. (2014). The cultural dimension of beliefs: An investigation of future primary teachers' epistemological beliefs concerning the nature of mathematics in 15 countries. In S. Blömeke, F.J. Hsieh, G. Kaiser, & W.H.Schmidt (Eds.), *International perspectives on teacher knowledge, beliefs and opportunities to learn* (pp. 209–29). Springer.

Ferris, D. R. (2001). Teaching writing for academic purposes. In J. Flowerdew & M. Peacock (Eds.), *Research perspectives on English for academic purposes* (pp. 298–314). Cambridge

University Press. https://doi.org/10.1017/CBO9781139524766
.023

Fiedler, L. A. (Ed.). (1981). *English literature: Opening up the canon. Selected papers from the English Institute, 1979*. Johns Hopkins University Press.

Fiel, J. E. (2020). Great equalizer or great selector? Reconsidering education as a moderator of intergenerational transmissions. *Sociology of Education*, *93*(4), 353–71. https://doi.org/10.1177
/0038040720927886

Fleetwood, L. (2022). *Science on the roof of the world: Empire and the remaking of the Himalaya*. Cambridge University Press.

Francis, B., Mills, M., & Lupton, R. (2017). Towards social justice in education: Contradictions and dilemmas. *Journal of Education Policy*, *32*(4), 414–31. https://doi.org/10.1080/02680939.2016
.1276218

Freire, P. (1968). *Pedagogy of the oppressed* (3rd ed.). Penguin Books.

Furlong, J. (2004). BERA at 30. Have we come of age? *British Educational Research Journal*, *30*(3), 343–58. https://doi.org/10
.1080/01411920410001689670

Furlong, J. (2013). *Education - An anatomy of the discipline. Rescuing the university project?* Routledge.

Garner, J. K., & Kaplan, A. (2019). A complex dynamic systems perspective on teacher learning and identity formation: An instrumental case. *Teachers and Teaching Theory and Practice*, *25*(1), 7–33. https://doi.org/10.1080/13540602.2018.1533811

Gauld, C. (2017). Democratising or privileging: The democratisation of knowledge and the role of the archivist. *Archival Science*, *17*(3), 227–45. https://doi.org/10.1007/s10502-015-9262-4

Geographical Association (2017). *Framework for enquiry*. https://
geography.org.uk/Framework-for-enquiry/

Gerrard, J., & Holloway, J. (2023). *Expertise: Keywords in teacher education*. Bloomsbury.

Gerrard, J., Sriprakash, A., & Rudolph, S. (2022). Education and racial capitalism. *Race Ethnicity and Education*, *25*(3), 425–42. https://doi.org/10.1080/13613324.2021.2001449

Gess-Newsome, J. (2015). Results of the thinking from the PCK summit. In A. Berry, P. Friedrichsen, & J. Loughran (Eds.), *Re-examining pedagogical content knowledge in science education* (pp. 28–42). Routledge.

Gettier, E. (1963). Is justified true belief knowledge? *Analysis*, *23*, 121–3.

Gibbons, S. (2019). 'Death by PEEL?' The teaching of writing in the secondary English classroom in England. *English in Education*, *53*(1), 36–45.

Gil-Perez, D., & Carrascosa, J. (1990). What to do about science 'misconceptions.' *Science Education*, *74*(5), 531–40.

Ginsburg, A., & Smith, M. S. (2016). *Do randomized controlled trials meet the 'gold standard'? A study of the usefulness of RCTs in the what works clearinghouse.* American Enterprise Institute.

Giovanelli, M., & Mason, J. (2015). 'Well I don't feel that': Schemas, worlds and authentic reading in the classroom. *English in Education*, *49*(1), 41–55. https://doi.org/10.1111/17548845.2015.11912523

Godfrey, D. (2016). Leadership of schools as research-led organisations in the English educational environment: Cultivating a research-engaged school culture. *Educational Management Administration & Leadership*, *44*(2), 301–21. https://doi.org/10.1177/1741143213508294

Goldacre, B. (2013). *Building evidence into education.* HMSO.

Graff, H. J. (2022). *Searching for literacy.* Palgrave Macmillan.

Gramsci, A. (1971). *Selection from the prison notebooks* (Q. Hoare & G. N. Smith, Eds.). Lawrence and Wishart.

Green, E. (2016). *What are the most-cited publications in the social sciences (according to Google Scholar)?* https://blogs.lse.ac.uk/impactofsocialsciences/2016/05/12/what-are-the-most-cited-publications-in-the-social-sciences-according-to-google-scholar/

Grimmet, P., & MacKinnon, A. (1992). Craft knowledge and the education of teachers. In G. Grant (Ed.), *Review of research in education.* Sage Publications Ltd. https://doi.org/10.3102/0091732X018001385

Guerriero, S. (Ed.). (2017). *Pedagogical knowledge and the changing nature of the teaching profession.* OECD Publishing. https://doi.org/10.1787/9789264270695-EN

Guilfoyle, L., McCormack, O., & Erduran, S. (2020). The 'tipping point' for educational research: The role of pre-service science teachers' epistemic beliefs in evaluating the professional utility of educational research. *Teaching and Teacher Education*, *90*, 103033. https://doi.org/10.1016/j.tate.2020.103033

Guillory, J. (1993). *Cultural capital: The problem of literary canon formation*. University of Chicago Press.

Hames-García, M. (2011). Queer theory revisited. In M. Hames-García & E. J. Martínez (Eds.), *Gay Latino studies: A critical reader* (pp. 19–45). Duke University Press.

Hands Up Education (2020). *Suburani*. Hands Up Education.

Healy, L., & Hoyles, C. (2000). A study of proof concepts in algebra. *Journal for Research in Mathematics Education*, *31*(4), 396–428. https://doi.org/10.2307/749651

Hirsch, E. D. (1987). *Cultural literacy: What every American needs to know*. Houghton Mifflin.

Hofer, B. K., & Pintrich, P.R. (1997). The development of epistemological theories: Beliefs about knowledge and knowing and their relation to learning. *Review of Educational Research*, *67*(1), 88–140.

Hollingsworth, S. (1989). Prior beliefs and cognitive change in learning to teach. *American Educational Research Journal*, *26*(2),160–89.

Holt-Reynolds, D. (1992). Personal history-based beliefs as relevant prior knowledge in course work. *American Educational Research Journal*, *29*(2), 325–49.

Hume, A., Cooper, R., & Borowski, A. (Eds.). (2019). *Repositioning pedagogical content knowledge in teachers' knowledge for teaching science*. Springer.

Ingram, J. (2018). Moving forward with ethnomethodological approaches to analysing mathematics classroom interactions. *ZDM – Mathematics Education*, *50*(6), 1065–75. https://doi.org/10.1007/s11858-018-0951-3

Ingram, J. (2020). Epistemic management in mathematics classroom interactions: Student claims of not knowing or not understanding. *Journal of Mathematical Behavior*, *58*(August 2019), 100754. https://doi.org/10.1016/j.jmathb.2019.100754

Ingram, J. (2021). *Patterns in mathematics classroom interaction: A conversation analytic approach*. Oxford University Press.

Ingram, J., & Andrews, N. (2019). What it means to do mathematics: The discursive construction of identities in the mathematics classroom. In M. Graven, H. Venkat, A. A. Essien, & P. Vale (Eds.), *Proceedings of the 43rd conference of the international group for the psychology of mathematics education* (Vol. 2, pp. 392–9). PME.

Ingram, J., & Andrews, N. (2020). Trying to improve communication skills: The challenge of joint sense making in classroom interactions. In *Proceedings of the seventh ERME topic conference on language in the mathematics classroom*, 155–62.

Ingram, J., Andrews, N., & Pitt, A. (2019). When students offer explanations without the teacher explicitly asking them to. *Educational Studies in Mathematics*, *101*(1), 51–66. https://doi.org/10.1007/s10649-018-9873-9

Ingram, J., & Gorgen, K. (2020). *TALIS video study: Case studies of mathematics teaching practices*. Department for Education.

Ingram, J., Pitt, A., & Baldry, F. (2015). Handling errors as they arise in whole-class interactions. *Research in Mathematics Education*, *17*(3), 183–97. https://doi.org/10.1080/14794802.2015.1098562

Ingram, J., & Riser, P. A. (2019). Experiences of problem solving in whole class interactions. *Avances de Investigación En Educación Matemática*, *November*, 5–21. https://doi.org/10.35763/aiem.v0i16.279

Inquiry Maths (n.d.). Retrieved 19 September 2022, from https://www.inquirymaths.com/

Jacobson, R., & Bialka, C. S. (2023). Identifying factors that promote or inhibit disability-related discussion in secondary English language arts classrooms. *English in Education*, *57*(3), 1–18. https://doi.org/10.1080/04250494.2023.2218879

Jazeel, T. (2019). *Postcolonialism*. Routledge. https://doi.org/10.4324/9781315559483

Jazeel, T. (2021). The 'city' as text. *International Journal of Urban and Regional Research*, *45*(4),658–62.

Kahneman, D. (2011). *Thinking, fast and slow*. MacMillan.

Kearns, G. (2009). *Geopolitics and empire: The legacy of Halford Mackinder*. Oxford University Press.

Kearns, G. (2020). Topple the racists 1: Decolonising the space and institutional memory of the university. *Geography*, *105*(3), 116–25. https://doi.org/10.1080/00167487.2020.12106473

Keats, J. (1977). *John Keats selected poems*. Edited and with an Introduction and Notes by John Barnard,edited by A. T. Quiller-Couch. Penguin.

Kennedy, M. M. (2004). Reform ideals and teachers' practical intentions. *Education Policy Analysis Archives*, *12*(13). https://doi.org/10.14507/epaa.v12n13.2004

Kenway, J., Fahey, J., Epstein, D., Koh, A., McCarthy, C., & Rizvi, F. (2017). *Class choreographies: Elite schools and globalization.* Palgrave Macmillan. https://doi.org/10.1057/978-1-137-54961-7 /COVER

Khoza, S. B., & Biyela, A. T. (2020). Decolonising technological pedagogical content knowledge of first year mathematics students. *Education and Information Technologies, 25*(4), 2665–79. https://doi.org/10.1007/S10639-019-10084-4/FIGURES/4

King, M. R., & chatGPT (2023). A conversation on artificial intelligence, chatbots, and plagiarism in higher education. *Cellular and Molecular Bioengineering, 16*(1), 1–2. https://doi.org /10.1007/s12195-022-00754-8

Lack, B. (2009). No excuses: A critique of the Knowledge in Power Program (KIPP) within charter schools in the USA. *Journal for Critical Education Policy Studies, 7*(2),126–53.

Lander, V. (2011). Race, culture and all that: An exploration of the perspectives of white secondary student teachers about race equality issues in their initial teacher education. *Race Ethnicity and Education, 14*(3), 351–64. https://doi.org/10.1080/13613324 .2010.543389

Lee, E., & Luft, J. A. (2008). Experienced secondary science teachers' representation of pedagogical content knowledge. *International Journal of Science Education, 30*(10), 1343–63. https://doi.org/10 .1080/09500690802187058

Lee, P., & Shemilt, D. (2009). Is any explanation better than none? Over-determined narratives, senseless agencies and one-way streets in students' learning about cause and consequence in history. *Teaching History, 137*, 42–9.

Lees, A., Ryan, A. M., Munoz, M., & Tocci, C. (2023). Mapping the indigenous postcolonial possibilities of teacher preparation. *Journal of Teacher Education*, 1–14. https://doi.org/10.1177 /00224871231199361

Lortie-Forgues, H., & Inglis, M. (2019). Rigorous large-scale educational RCTs are often uninformative: Should we be concerned? *Educational Researcher, 48*(3), 158–66. https://doi .org/10.3102/0013189X19832850

Lynch, C., & Rata, E. (2018). Culturally responsive pedagogy: A New Zealand case study. *International Studies in Sociology of Education, 27*(4), 391–408. https://doi.org/10.1080/09620214 .2018.1468274

Macaluso, M., & Macaluso, K. (Eds.). (2018). *Teaching the canon in 21st century classrooms: Challenging genres*. Brill.

MacDonald, L., & Kidman, J. (2022). Uncanny pedagogies: Teaching difficult histories at sites of colonial violence. *Critical Studies in Education*, *63*(1), 31–46. https://doi.org/10.1080/17508487.2021.1923543

Maggioni, L., & Parkinson, M. M. (2008). The role of teacher epistemic cognition, epistemic beliefs, and calibration in instruction. *Educational Psychology Review*, *20*(4), 445–61.

Mairiga, N., & Ibrahim, M. (2021). Assessment of indigenous knowledge in managing environmental challenges: A case study of Ringim local government area of Jigawa State,Nigeria. *International Journal of Scientific Advances*, *2*(4), 606–11. https://doi.org/10.51542/ijscia.v2i4.25

Marrun, N. A., Clark, C., Beach, K., Morgan, M., Lopez-Chaing, C., Gonzalez, C., & McCadney, O. (2023). Indifferent, (Un) critical, and anti-intellectual: Framing how teachers grapple with bans on teaching truth about race and racism, and critical race theory. *Race, Ethnicity and Education*, https://doi.org/10.1080/13613324.2023.2203935

Mason, J., Burton, L., & Stacey, K. (2010). *Thinking mathematically* (2nd ed.). Pearson. https://doi.org/10.12968/eyed.2013.15.2.18

Mason, J., & Spence, M. (1999). Beyond mere knowledge of mathematics: The importance of knowing-to act in the moment. *Educational Studies in Mathematics*, *38*(1), 135–61. https://doi.org/10.1023/A:1003622804002

McGann, M., Ryan, M., Mcmahon, J., & Hall, T. (n.d.). *T-REX: The teachers' research exchange. Overcoming the research-practice gap in education*. https://doi.org/10.1007/s11528-020-00486-4

McGowan, T. (2001). *Feminine 'No!': Psychoanalysis and the new cannon*. State University of New York Press.

McGowan, T. (2014). *Feminine 'No!':Psychoanalysis and the new canon*. State University of New York Press.

McIntyre, D. (1995). Initial teacher education as practical theorising: A response to Paul Hirst. *British Journal of Educational Studies*, *43*(4), 365–83.

McIntyre, J., & Hobson, A. J. (2016). Supporting beginner teacher identity development: External mentors and the third space. *Research Papers in Education*, *31*(2), 133–58. https://doi.org/10.1080/02671522.2015.1015438

McKittrick, K. (2021). *Dear science and other stories*. Duke University Press.

McLean Davies, L., Doecke, B., Mead, P., Sawyer, W., & Yates, L. (Eds.). (2023). *Literary knowing and the making of English teachers: The role of literature in shaping English teachers' professional knowledge and identities*. Routledge. https://www.routledge.com/Literary-Knowing-and-the-Making-of-English-Teachers-The-Role-of-Literature/Davies-Doecke-Mead-Sawyer-Yates/p/book/9780367618681

McLean Davies, L., Martin, S. K., & Buzacott, L. (2022). Critical considerations of the challenges of teaching national literatures in Australia in the 21st century. *The Australian Educational Researcher*, *49*, 463–79. https://doi.org/10.1007/s13384-021-00448-6

McPhail, G., & Rata, E. (2016). Comparing curriculum types: 'Powerful Knowledge' and '21st Century Learning'. *New Zealand Journal of Educational Studies*, *51*, 53–68. https://doi.org/10.1007/s40841-015-0025-9

Mignolo, W. D. (2011). *The darker side of Western modernity: Global futures, decolonial options*. Duke University Press.

Mincu, M., & Davies, P. (2019). The governance of a school network and implications for initial teacher education. *Journal of Education Policy*, *36*(3), 436–53.

Ministry of Education (2021). *Te Hurihanganui*. https://www.education.govt.nz/our-work/overall-strategies-and-policies/te-hurihanganui/

Mika, C. (2017). *Indigenous education and the metaphysics of presence: A worlded philosophy*.Taylor & Francis.

Morgan, B., West, E. G., Nakata, M., Hall, K., Swisher, K., Ahenakew, F., Hughes, P., Ka'ai, T., & Blair,N. (1999). The Coolangatta statement on Indigenous rights in education. *Journal of American Indian Education*, *39*(1),52–64.

Mori, C., & Davies, I. (2015). Citizenship education in civics textbooks in the Japanese junior high school curriculum. *Asia Pacific Journal of Education*, *35*(2), 153–75. https://doi.org/10.1080/02188791.2014.959468

Mork, S. M., Haug, B. S., Sørborg, Ø., Parameswaran Ruben, S., & Erduran, S. (2022). Humanising the nature of science: An analysis of the science curriculum in Norway. *International Journal of*

Science Education, *44*(10), 1601–18. https://doi.org/10.1080/09500693.2022.2088876

Morrison, G. R., Ross, S. M., Gopalakrishnan, M., & Casey, J. (1995). The effects of feedback and incentives on achievement in computer-based instruction. *Contemporary Educational Psychology*, *20*(1), 32–50. https://doi.org/10.1006/CEPS.1995.1002

Muller, J., & Young,M. (2019). Knowledge, power and powerful knowledge re-visited. *Curriculum Journal*, *30*(2), 196–214.

Newmann, F. M., & Archbald, D. A. (1992). The nature of authentic academic achievement. In *Toward a new science of educational testing and assessment* (pp. 71–83). State University of New York Press.

Newton, L. D., & Newton, D.P. (2008). To what extent can children's geography books help a primary school teacher explain cause and purpose? *International Research in Geographical and Environmental Education*, *15*(1),29–40.

Noble, S. U. (2018). *Algorithms of oppression: How search engines reinforce racism.* New York University Press. https://doi.org/10.18574/nyu/9781479833641.001.0001

Norcup, J. (2015). *Awkward geographies? An historical and cultural geography of the journal Contemporary Issues in Geography and Education (CIGE) (1983–1991).* University of Glasgow. http://geography.exeter.ac.uk/staff/index.php?web_id=Ian_Cook

OECD. (n.d.). *PISA - PISA.* Retrieved 19 September 2022, from https://www.oecd.org/pisa/

OECD (1996). *The knowledge-based economy* (pp. 1–). OECD.

OFS. (2022). Setting our future direction. https://www.officeforstudents.org.uk/news-blog-and-events/blog/setting-our-future-direction/

Ofsted (2019). *School inspection update* (Issue January). HMSO.

Ofsted (2021). *Research review series: Geography.* https://www.gov.uk/government/publications/research-review-series-geography

Ofsted (2023). Initial teacher education (ITE) inspection framework and handbook (updated 14 July 2023). Retrieved 10 October 2023, from https://www.gov.uk/government/publications/initial-teacher-education-ite-inspection-framework-and-handbook/initial-teacher-education-ite-inspection-framework-and-handbook-for-september-2023

Olsen, B. (2014). Learning from experience: A teacher-identity perspective. In V. Ellis & J. Orchard (Eds.), *Learning teaching from experience: Multiple perspectives and international contexts* (pp. 79–94). Bloomsbury.

Olufemi, L. (2019). Academic and unbearable whiteness. In O. Younge (Ed.), *A fly girl's guide to university* (pp. 56–8). Verve Words.

Orchard, J., & Winch, C. (2015). What training do teachers need? *Impact*, *2015*(22), 1–43.

Patel, L. (2014). Countering coloniality in educational research: From ownership to answerability. *Educational Studies*, *50*(4), 357–77. https://doi.org/10.1080/00131946.2014.924942

Patel, L. (2016). *Decolonizing educational research: From ownership to answerability*. Routledge. https://www.routledge.com/Decolonizing-Educational-Research-From-Ownership-to-Answerability/Patel/p/book/9781138998728

Penuel, W. R., Allen, A. R., Coburn, C. E., & Farrell, C. (2015). Conceptualizing research–practice partnerships as joint work at boundaries. *Journal of Education for Students Placed at Risk*, *20*(1–2), 182–97. https://doi.org/10.1080/10824669.2014.988334

Perry, M. (2000). Explanations of mathematical concepts in Japanese, Chinese, and U.S. first-and fifth-grade classrooms. *Cognition and Instruction*, *18*(2), 181–207. https://doi.org/10.1207/S1532690XCI1802_02

Perry, T., Lea, R., Jørgensen, C. R., Cordingley, P., Shapiro, K., & Youdell, D. (2021). *Cognitive science in the classroom: Evidence and practice review*. Education Endowment Foundation. https://d2tic4wvo1iusb.cloudfront.net/documents/guidance/Cognitive_Science_in_the_classroom_-_Evidence_and_practice_review.pdf?v=1681842605

Peterson, S. M., & French, L. (2008). Supporting young children's explanations through inquiry science in preschool. *Early Childhood Research Quarterly*, *23*(3), 395–408.

Pickles, E. (2011). Assessment of students' uses of evidence: Shifting the focus from processes to historical reasoning. *Teaching History*, *143*, 52–9.

Propp, J. (2021). *Why names matter*. Mathematical Enchantments. https://mathenchant.wordpress.com/2021/11/16/why-names-matter/

Puttick, S. (2015). *Geography teachers' subject knowledge: An ethnographic study of three secondary school geography departments*. University of Oxford.

Puttick, S. (2018). Student teachers' positionalities as knowers in school subject departments. *British Educational Research Journal*, 44(1), 25–42. https://doi.org/10.1002/berj.3314

Puttick, S., Chandrachud, P., Chopra, R., Khosla, R., Robson, J., Singh, S., & Talks, I. (2022). Climate change education: Following the information. In L. Hammond, M. Biddulph, S. Catling, & J. H. Mcendrick (Eds.), *Children, education and geography: Rethinking intersections*. Routledge.

Puttick, S., & Murrey, A. (2020). Confronting the deafening silence on race in geography education in England: Learning from anti-racist, decolonial and black geographies. *Geography*, 105(3), 126–34. https://doi.org/10.1080/00167487.2020.12106474

Puttick, S., & Warren-Lee, N. (2021). Geography mentors' written lesson observation feedback during initial teacher education. *International Research in Geographical and Environmental Education*, 30(2), 95–111. https://doi.org/10.1080/10382046.2020.1757830

Puttick, S., & Wynn, J. (2021). Constructing 'good teaching' through written lesson observation feedback. *Oxford Review of Education*, 47(2), 152–69. https://doi.org/10.1080/03054985.2020.1846289

Rabinowitz, N. S., & McHardy, F. (2014). *From abortion to pederasty: Addressing difficult topics in the classics classroom*. The Ohio State University Press.

Raffles, T. S. S. (1819). *Minute by Sir T.S. Raffles on the establishment of a Malay College at Singapore*.

Rata, E. (2022). The decolonisation of education in New Zealand, breaking views. New Zealand Centre for Political Research. https://breakingviewsnz.blogspot.com/2022/04/elizabeth-rata-decolonisation-of.html

Rinne, R., & Ozga, J. (2020). The OECD and the global re-regulation of teachers' work: Knowledge-based regulation tools and teachers in Finland and England. In T. Seddon & J. Levin (Eds.), *World yearbook of education 2013: Educators, professionalism and politics: Global transitions, national spaces and professional projects* (pp. 117–36). Taylor & Francis Group. https://doi.org/10.4324/9780203073940-16

Rivera, F. A. G., Rios, M. C., Freedman, B. F., & Rahman, E. A. (2023). Formabiap's indigenous educative community, Peru: A biosocial pedagogy. *Oxford Review of Education, 49*(5). https://doi.org/forthcoming

Roberts, M. (2013). *Geography through enquiry: Approaches to teaching and learning in the secondary school.* Geographical Association.

Rose, G. (2020). Editorial introduction by Professor Gillian Rose: Diversity and inclusion. *Routes Journal, 1*(2), 139–41.

Roth, K. R., & Ritter, Z. S. (Eds.). (2021). *Whiteness, power, and resisting change in US higher education: A peculiar institution.* Palgrave Macmillan.

Rowland, C. A. (2014). The effect of testing versus restudy on retention: A meta-analytic review of the testing effect. *Psychological Bulletin, 140*(6), 1432–63. https://doi.org/10.1037/a0037559

Rowland, T., Huckstep, P., & Thwaites, A. (2005). Elementary teachers' mathematics subject knowledge: The knowledge quartet and the case of Naomi. *Journal of Mathematics Teacher Education, 8*(3), 255–81. https://doi.org/10.1007/s10857-005-0853-5

Rudolph, S., Sriprakash, A., & Gerrard, J. (2018). Knowledge and racial violence: The shine and shadow of 'powerful knowledge'. *Ethics and Education, 13*(1), 22–38. https://doi.org/10.1080/17449642.2018.1428719

Santoro, N., Reid, J. A., Mayer, D., & Singh, M. (2013). Teacher knowledge: Continuing professional learning. *Asia-Pacific Journal of Teacher Education, 41*(2), 123–5. https://doi.org/10.1080/1359866X.2013.777326

Sawyer, W., & McLean Davies, L. (2021). What do we want students to know from being taught a poem? *Changing English, 28*(1), 103–17. https://doi.org/10.1080/1358684X.2020.1842174

Schack, E. O., Fisher, M. H., & Wilhelm, J.A. (Eds.). (2017). *Teacher noticing: Bridging and broadening perspectives, contexts, and frameworks (Research in Mathematics Education).* Springer.

Scheiner, T., Montes, M. A., Godino, J. D., Carrillo, J., & Pino-Fan, L. R. (2019). What makes mathematics teacher knowledge specialized? Offering alternative views. *International Journal of Science and Mathematics Education, 17*, 153–72. https://doi.org/10.1007/s10763-017-9859-6

Schmid, M., Brianza, E., & Petko, D. (2020). Developing a short assessment instrument for Technological Pedagogical Content Knowledge (TPACK.xs) and comparing the factor structure of an integrative and a transformative model. *Computers & Education*, *157*, 103967. https://doi.org/10.1016/J.COMPEDU .2020.103967

Schoenfeld, A. H. (1985). *Mathematical problem solving*. Academic Press.

Schön, D. A. (1983). *The reflective practitioner: How professionals think in action*. Basic Books.

Schraw, G., Olafson, L., & Vander Veldt, M. (2012). Fostering critical awareness of teachers' Epistemological and ontological beliefs. In J. Brownlee, G. Schraw, & D.Berthelsen (Eds.), *Personal epistemology and teacher education* (pp. 61–149). Routledge.

Seeley, J. R. (1870). *Lectures and essays*. Macmillan.

Seixas, P., & Morton, T. (2013). *The big six: Historical thinking concepts*. Nelson Education.

Seow, T., Irvine, K. N., Beevi, I., & Premathillake, T. (2020). Field-based enquiry in geography: The influence of Singapore teachers' subject identities on their practice. *International Research in Geographical and Environmental Education*, *29*(4), 347–61. https://doi.org/10.1080/10382046.2019.1680001

Settlage, J. (2013). On acknowledging PCK's shortcomings. *Journal of Science Teacher Education*, *24*(1), 1–12. https://doi.org/10 .1007/s10972-012-9332-x

Shulman, L. S. (1986). Those who understand: Knowledge growth in teaching. *Educational Researcher*, *15*(2), 4–14. https://doi.org/10 .3102/0013189X015002004

Sinclair, N., Healy, L., & Sales, C. O. R. (2009). Time for telling stories: Narrative thinking with dynamic geometry. *ZDM - The International Journal on Mathematics Education*, *41*, 441–52. https://doi.org/10.1007/s11858-009-0180-x

Smith, C. A., & Garrett-Scott, D. (2021). 'We are not named': Black women and the politics of citation in anthropology. *Feminist Anthropology*, *2*(1), 18–37. https://doi.org/10.1002/FEA2.12038

Smith III, J. P., DiSessa, A. A., & Roschelle, J. (1994). Misconceptions reconceived: A constructivist analysis of knowledge in transition. *The Journal of the Learning Sciences*, *3*(2), 115–63. https://doi.org/10.1207/s15327809jls0302_1

Snapper, G. (2009). Beyond English literature a level: The silence of the seminar? *English in Education*, *43*(3), 192–210. https://doi.org/10.1111/17548845.2009.11912389

SoGE (2019). *Oxford geography's uncomfortable history*. https://www.geog.ox.ac.uk/news/2019/1023-mackinder-gerry-kearns.html

Sriprakash, A., Rudolph, S., & Gerrard, J. (2021). *Learning whiteness: Education and the settler colonial state*. Pluto Press.

Swan, M. (2008). Designing a multiple representation learning experience in secondary algebra. *Educational Designer*, *1*(1), 1–17.

Taylor, C. (1994). The politics of recognition. In A. Gutmann (Ed.), *Multiculturalism: Examining the politics of recognition* (pp. 25–73). Princeton University Press.

Terrin, É., & Triventi, M. (2022). The effect of school tracking on student achievement and inequality: A meta-analysis. *Review of Educational Research*. https://doi.org/10.3102/00346543221100850

Tirosh, D., Tsamir, P., Levenson, E., & Tabach, M. (2011). From preschool teachers' professional development to children's knowledge: Comparing sets. *Journal of Mathematics Teacher Education*, *14*(2), 113–31. https://doi.org/10.1007/s10857-011-9172-1

Todd, Z. (2016). An indigenous feminist's take on the ontological turn: 'ontology' is just another word for colonialism. *Journal of Historical Sociology*, *29*(1), 4–22. https://doi.org/10.1111/johs.12124

Trudgill, S., & Roy, A. (Eds.). (2003). *Contemporary meanings in physical geography: From what to why?* Routledge. https://doi.org/10.4324/9780203784044

Trudgill, S. T. (2003). Meaning, knowledge, constructs and fieldwork in physical geography. In S. T. Trudgill & A. Roy (Eds.), *Contemporary meanings in physical geography: From what to why?* Routledge. https://doi.org/10.4324/9780203784044-3

Tuhiwai Smith, L. (2021). *Decolonizing methodologies: Research and indigenous peoples*. Bloomsbury Publishing.

van Deur, P., & Murray-Harvey, R. (2005). The inquiry nature of primary schools and students' self-directed learning knowledge. *International Education Journal*, *5*(5), 166–77.

van Drie, J., & van Boxtel, C. (2008). Historical reasoning: Towards a framework for analyzing students' reasoning about the past. *Educational Psychology Review, 20*(2), 87–110. https://doi.org/10.1007/s10648-007-9056-1

Vass, G., & Hogarth, M. (2022). Can we keep up with the aspirations of Indigenous education? *Critical Studies in Education, 63*(1),1–14. https://doi.org/10.1080/17508487.2022.2031617

Walford, R. (2001). *Geography in British schools, 1850–2000: Making a world of difference.* Woburn.

Wang, Z., Liu, J., Xu, N., Fan, C., Fan, Y., He, S., Jiao, L., & Ma,N. (2019). The role of indigenous knowledge in integrating scientific and indigenous knowledge for community-based disaster risk reduction: A case of Haikou Village in Ningxia, China. *International Journal of Disaster Risk Reduction, 41*, 101309. https://doi.org/10.1016/j.ijdrr.2019.101309

Watson, A. (2008). School mathematics as a special kind of mathematics. *For the Learning of Mathematics, 28*(3), 3–7.

Welch, S. (2019). Native epistemology and embodied cognitive theory. In S. Welch (Ed.), *The phenomenology of a performative knowledge system* (pp. 53–89). Palgrave Macmillan. https://doi.org/10.1007/978-3-030-04936-2_3

Wendell, J. (2020). Qualifying counterfactuals: Students' use of counterfactuals for evaluating historical explanations. *History Education Research Journal, 17*(1), 50–66.

White, J. (2018). The weakness of 'powerful knowledge'. *London Review of Education, 16*(2), 325–35. https://doi.org/10.18546/LRE.16.2.11

White, J. (2019). The end of powerful knowledge? *London Review of Education, 17*(3), 429–38. https://doi.org/10.18546/LRE.17.3.15

Williams, R. (1985). *Keywords: A vocabulary of culture and society.* Oxford University Press.

Wilson, A., & Laing,M. (2018). Queering indigenous education. In L. Tuhiwai Smith, E. Tuck, & K. W.Yang (Eds.), *Indigenous and decolonizing studies in education: Mapping the long view.* Routledge.

Winch, C., Oancea, A., & Orchard, J. (2015). The contribution of educational research to teachers' professional learning: Philosophical understandings. *Oxford Review of Education, 41*(2), 202–16. https://doi.org/10.1080/03054985.2015.1017406

Wineburg, S. S. (2018). *Why learn history (when it's already on your phone)*. The University of Chicago Press.

Wittgenstein, L. (1958). *Philosophical Investigations* (2nd ed.). Basil Blackwell.

Wyse, D., & Bradbury, A. (2022). Reading wars or reading reconciliation? A critical examination of robust research evidence, curriculum policy and teachers' practices for teaching phonics and reading. *Review of Education, 10*(1), 1–35. https://doi.org/10.1002/rev3.3314

Yackel, E., & Cobb, P. (1996). Sociomathematical norms, argumentation, and autonomy in mathematics. *Journal for Research in Mathematics Education, 27*(4), 458–77.

Yang, L., Marginson, S., & Xu, X. (2022). 'Thinking through the world': A tianxia heuristic for higher education. *Globalisation, Societies and Education*, 1–17. https://doi.org/10.1080/14767724.2022.2098696

Young, M. (2013a). Overcoming the crisis in curriculum theory: A knowledge-based approach. *Journal of Curriculum Studies, 45*(2), 101–18. https://doi.org/10.1080/00220272.2013.764505

Young, M. (2013b). Powerful knowledge: An analytically useful concept or just a 'sexy sounding term'? A response to John Beck's 'Powerful knowledge, esoteric knowledge, curriculum knowledge'. *Cambridge Journal of Education, 43*(2), 195–8. https://doi.org/10.1080/0305764X.2013.776356

Young, M. F. D. (1971). *Knowledge and control: New directions for the sociology of education*. MacMillan.

Young, M. F. D. (2000). Rescuing the sociology of educational knowledge from the extremes of voice discourse: Towards a new theoretical basis for the sociology of the curriculum. *British Journal of Sociology of Education, 21*(4), 523–36. https://doi.org/10.1080/713655366

Young, M. F. D. (2008). *Bringing knowledge back in: From social constructivism to social realism in the sociology of education*. Routledge.

Young, M., & Lambert, D. (2014). *Knowledge and the future school: Curriculum and social justice*. Bloomsbury Academic.

Young, M., Lambert, D., Roberts, C., & Roberts, M. (2014). *Knowledge and the future school: Curriculum and social justice*. Bloomsbury.

Young, M., & Muller, J. (2013). On the powers of powerful knowledge. *Review of Education*, *1*(3), 229–50. https://doi.org/10.1002/rev3.3017

Zagzebski, L. (1999). What is knowledge? In J. Greco & E. Sosa (Eds.), *The blackwell guide to epistemology* (pp. 92–116). Blackwell Publishers Ltd. https://doi.org/10.1111/b.9780631202912.1998.x

Zaslavsky, O. (2005). Seizing the opportunity to create uncertainty in learning mathematics. *Educational Studies in Mathematics*, *60*(3), 297–321. https://doi.org/10.1007/s10649-005-0606-5

Zazkis, R., & Mamolo, A. M. I. (2011). Reconceptualizing knowledge at the mathematical horizon. *For the Learning of Mathematics*, *31*(2), 8–13.

INDEX